[2022] [Puppy Information Course Book ©SuzanneManRay2018

PUPPY SUPPORT BOOK

TRAINING AND INFORMATION

PUPPY TRAINING

A 6-Week Course and Puppy Info Book written by Suzanne Man-Ray

This Puppy Guide and 6 Week Puppy Course book has been designed with both you, the dog owner and your puppy's relationship, as well as communication in mind. It is a guide of what we will cover with you during our 6 Week Puppy Course together if you have booked in-person support. Supporting you, your puppy, and the whole family during early development of your new companion. The puppy book outlines what you will cover with us with broken down steps for each behaviour to follow, plus tips and information to help you through puppy development and adolescence. The book can be also followed from home.

Where teaching life skills builds confidence and relationships!

CONTENTS

Page No.

Reward-Based Training…………………………………………………4

The First Weeks with your Puppy………………………………………5-6

Toilet Training…………………………………………………………6-7

Canine Companions and Sentient Beings…………………………………8

Dog Enrichment and the World of Scent…………………………………9-10

Puppy Class 6-Week Plan……………………………………………11-13

Week One:

Safe Exercise for Puppies…………………………………………14-15

What is Socialisation?……………………………………………15-16

Fireworks and Sound Sensitivity………………………………………17-19

Puppy and Dog Behaviour……………………………………………20-21

Socialisation and Dog Body Language………………………………21-23

Dog's and Children……………………………………………………23-24

Desensitisation………………………………………………………25

Dog Law………………………………………………………………26-28

Local Dog Information…………………………………………………29

Harness, Lead and Collar Desensitisation and Equipment………30-31

Shaping, using a Clicker or marker word…………………………31-33

Crate/Confinement Training……………………………………………33-34

Puppy Biting…………………………………………………………34-35

Nutrition………………………………………………………………35-36

Week Two: Getting Puppy Skills Started

Food Manners……………………………………………………………37

Jumping Up……………………………………………………………37-38

TRAINING & BONDING TIPS

Long lasting treats like frozen Kong's, natural chews, chew roots, age-appropriate half antlers all aid in calming and help with teething.

Freeze Kong's filled with goats yoghurt which is low in lactose for more sensitive dogs, natural yoghurt or Primula squeezy cheese.

A frozen or filled treat will be long lasting reinforcement for settling on mat, bed, or blanket. Something prepared and taken out with you.

Teaching a Drop...38-39

Settling...39-40

Week Three: Recall Week

Reflex to Name..41-42

Charging the Recall Cue...42

Counting Game and Recall Games...43-44

Hand Target..45-46

Week Four: Cues to keep your Puppy safe

Teaching a Stay..46-47

Door and Gate Safety..48

Teaching a Leave...48-49

Loose Lead Foundations...49-50

Week Five: Husbandry and Cooperative Care

The Bucket Game...51-52

Teaching A Stand...52-54

Beginning Muzzle Training...54-55

Loose Lead Skills...56-57

Week Six: Building Our Puppy Skills

Practising Recall Skills...58

Loose Lead Walking..58

The Backpack Walk..59-60

Cues and Behaviours..61-63

Weekly Puppy Training Schedules..64-71

About the Author..72

References and Notes...73-74

REWARD BASED TRAINING

Positive Reinforcement (R+) is a type of learning method (Operant Conditioning, discovered by B.F. Skinner), where we add a stimulus that increases the likelihood of a wanted behaviour being repeated. There are 4 quadrants involved in operant learning: positive reinforcement, negative reinforcement, positive punishment and negative punishment. Each of these quadrants ends with a consequence that can make the behaviour more or less likely.

Positive Reinforcement is based on motivation and enjoyment which naturally leads to happy learning experiences and is used in classroom teaching environments in schools. This method also builds a positive relationship between a dog and their owner. We use positive reinforcement in training to not only reinforce desired behaviours, but also in regard to a dog's brain chemistry. Experiences that produce a positive response will cause the brain's reward area and activation of the neurotransmitter dopamine. This biological event aids motivation and memory so the dog learns, remembers, and enjoys the experience.

Positive Reinforcement means that we add something the dog finds rewarding/pleasant to a situation when a dog is carrying out a behaviour which we would like them to repeat. This works when timed and paired with a wanted behaviour. Wait for your dog to offer a behaviour you want, then reward with a treat or toy your dog likes. A few repetitions of this when the dog makes the link between the behaviour and the treat, will create a very solid behaviour that the dog will begin to offer, in case there is the chance of a reward. Once the behaviour is consistent you can then add a verbal or physical cue for the specific behaviour.

Learning and the 3 'D's: The key to teaching and likewise learning, is to move at the learner's pace and slowly build new behaviours. Dog trainers will often speak about the "three Ds" in training: duration, distance, and distraction. Each of these represents a set of challenges for the dog. Gradually increasing the criteria, the time you ask the dog for a behaviour, for example a 'touch', then marking that duration with a click or marker word, adding your reinforcement (reward) increases duration. (Food for e.g.) Distance we increase by slowly moving away from the dog and asking for the 'touch' behaviour. We can add distraction by practising in different environments. We always raise our criteria by changing 1 'D' at a time. So, if increasing duration, practice in a quiet, known environment for success in training.

TRAINING & BONDING TIPS

We train our dogs on non-slip mats for a few reasons. Firstly, to prevent injury on hard flooring and secondly the mat acts as a start signal for training for the dogs.

The dog's consent to training by moving to their mat. When they move away from the mat, training stops.

Our training mats have a positive association which has been built. The mat represents fun time and play with us and yummy rewards.

THE FIRST WEEKS WITH YOUR PUPPY

We recommend puppy sleeps with/near you during early development. A few days earlier your puppy was reliant on his mother and siblings for warmth, security, play and companionship. Leaving a puppy to 'cry it out' away from you creates stress and a feeling of helplessness, (Seligman, 1972). This can impact puppies neurologically, cause anxiety and lose confidence (Panksepp et al, 1978). More recent studies have also shown that dogs have an area in the brain responsible for feeling emotion, hence we need to be aware of how emotion drives behaviour. (Berns. G, 2020) A puppy left to cry at night, may stop crying after a few days, but this will be due to shutting down, knowing no one will come to their cry and are abandoned. You are now their family and want a close bond and relationship built on trust and care. Having this bond and offering comfort will lead to a confident and happy dog.

Reflex to Name

We want your dog to associate their name you have chosen with the positive and good things. Teaching your dog to recognise and respond to his/her name is for focus and eye contact with you. Always say their name in a happy positive tone to create a positive association.

'Dog's Name': (Reflex to Name/Word (turn of the head, check in, eye contact)) **= Reward** (Drop treats next to you or give your dog a treat, this will also help recall skills.)

A reflex to name can be practiced at home, whilst walking on lead or at a distance, we are just asking for eye contact/engagement/check. As soon as your dog's eyes or head move upwards or towards you, reward with a treat immediately. This will create an immediate positive feeling to their name and associate good things

A Puppy's Space

It is important to consider what puppy proofed space your puppy will have access too during the day. Think about what behaviour you do want to see and set your puppy up for success in your home. An area that is safe, small and has water, a comfortable bed, settle blankets and appropriate chews and toys. We need to focus on teaching our puppies wanted behaviours, settling, appropriate play, encourage chewing and licking for example. Some puppy owners use a pen which gives a puppy choice but is also a safe secure space. Think about items left out as well, a puppy will not differentiate between your shoes or remote control and puppy chew. We can also guarantee there is likely to be something chewed however! The better you puppy proof, moving things off surfaces, making sure wires are safely hidden to putting shoes away you are setting up puppy for success and saving your items from puppy teeth. Puppies grow very fast so you will need to continuously change your puppy proofing as your puppy becomes bigger, more energetic, and more mobile.

First Nights/Overnight

Young puppies and often rescue dogs will need to go to the toilet once or twice in the night for anything from a few days to a number of weeks or months. Having your puppy near your, either in your bed or in a bed next to you, will make it much easier for you to know when they need the toilet. Have some slippers or slip-on shoes next to the bed to slip on and carry your puppy downstairs to the garden. You must never deny your dog water (Under the 5 Freedoms, Animal Welfare). Fresh water must be always available, so a tray with your puppy's water dish in next to your bed will help with spillages. Likewise, an attached bowl within a crate if you choose to crate train. Remember that crate training is teaching your puppy/dog to feel relaxed and settled in a confined space, but is not toilet training, or teaching your puppy about how to behave in our human spaces. Denying a dog or puppy of water does not aid toilet training. It will affect your dog's health and could lead to urinary infections and other complications.

Toilet Training

Toilet training is easy to train if you are consistent. Young puppies have very small bladders and little bladder control due to maturity and development, which can take a year or longer to mature. Rescue dogs have often been kept in small indoor spaces with no other area to toilet. Therefore, it is our responsibility to make sure our puppy or dog is in the right area outside to toilet.

Toilet Breaks

- When your puppy wakes up from a nap or night's sleep.
- After playtime, activity, or a training session.
- After every meal.
- After drinking water.
- When you come home.
- Before you leave the home.
- Before bedtime.
- And every twenty to thirty minutes during the day unless they are asleep. During periods of activity, change the schedule to every ten to twenty minutes.

Our Puppy and Dog Carer's Job

Stay outside with your puppy while they sniff and gently wander. Should your puppy be apprehensive about going into the garden, encourage them with some treats. You can crumble some into the grass for your puppy to naturally sniff. This will encourage your dog to go to the toilet. You can gently praise your puppy and if you want to add a cue, for example, 'Go Wee' or 'Toilet'.

After your puppy has finished going to the toilet head back inside. If you continue playing a game or some outside training remember to wait for your puppy to toilet once more before going back indoors. If you are feeling frustrated go back inside and then try again a 5/10 minutes later. We don't want to set your puppy or dog up to fail. Puppies will have accidents, but this is due to us not toilet training them yet or seeing the signs they need to go.

Get to know your dog's body language, watch their subtle body movements, circling and sniffing which are some of the signs a dog is about to toilet. If you have an older dog that has been previously toilet trained and begins to toilet inside, we advise you to seek veterinary advice. Some health issues can cause bladder and bowl problems. With all behaviour changes always consult a veterinary professional.

Tips

- Don't use puppy training pads or newspaper. This will confuse your puppy as they will see these areas as a place to toilet and make teaching your dog to toilet in the garden much harder.

- Don't leave the door open. This doesn't teach a dog that the garden is where to toilet.

- No punishment when your puppy has an accident. Harsh words will damage your bond, your dog will not relate punishment to where he went to the toilet, not just the act itself.

- Don't expect your puppy to let you know when he/she needs to relieve themself. A plan of regular toilet breaks will speed up the toilet training. (We can show you how to use training bells at the door once toilet training has begun.)

- Do not scold or punish your dog for accidents inside. This can lead to you dogs still toileting inside the home whilst you are not present due to stress or fear, trying to hide toileting from you.

Note: Areas indoors where your puppy or dog has had an accident are best cleaned with either biological washing powder or a kennel cleaner from your local pet store. Avoid using disinfectant as this contains ammonia and can encourage pup to toilet there again.

Chewing and Licking:

Licking: like chewing is a natural behaviour which you can encourage with filled yummy Kongs, Lickimats filled with dog peanut butter and long-lasting treats work well. Look for Lickimats on Amazon for great prices. https://www.industripet.com/product-category/lickimats/

Chews: Increase variety in chews, chewing is a natural behaviour like scent and tapping into this will also help her ability to relax in different environments. Chew roots and natural age-appropriate chews. We highly recommend either visiting or looking online at this store for great ideas for treats and chews. In store the owners offer great advice too. https://www.naturaltreatsbristol.co.uk/

Puppy Training Equipment Recommendations:

- Soft Puppy Harness (Most pet stores will carry soft small harnesses.)
- Multi clip lead: Walking Lead for Dogs. Available in different sizes and colours https://swaggerpaws.com/collections/dog-leads
- 5 metre biothane long line: Perfect for Recall Training, and management whilst training, Available in 5m and 10m https://swaggerpaws.com/collections/all/products/waterproof-long-line-leads-large
- Puppy Bag: Portable bowl, fresh water, Lickimat, Kong, Blanket, poo bags, Primula squeezy cheese.
- Treat bag: These can be on a belt or attachable. Available online and in pet stores.
- A blanket or mat for settling and capturing calm.

Canine Companions and Sentient Beings

Our canine companions have the same range of emotions of a 2-year-old human child. Dogs have the same brain structure as a human, that produces emotions as well as the same hormones and chemical changes. The hormone oxytocin is also present in dogs. Which in humans is involved in affection and the feeling of love. (Coren. S; 2013, Psychology Today)

Young children have a limited range of emotions, however over time and development the child's emotions begin to develop and they are able to experience different and complex emotions. Not all people have a full range of possible emotions, and this research helps us understand the emotional side of our domestic dogs. Complex social emotions that require learning do not appear until later, for example shame, pride and guilt. These more complex emotions a dog does not experience. Though currently there are further research projects to identify further emotions in animals.

Due to research, we know that the emotions available to a dog will not exceed that of a 2 to 2.5-year-old human child, this means that a dog will have the basic emotions of joy, fear, disgust and love. This information is important for dog behaviourists and trainers, especially knowing that a dog does not feel guilt. For example, when a puppy toilets on the floor in the home, he may exhibit body language that we may interpret as guilty, however this is not guilt but the more basic emotion of fear. Your annoyed, frustrated presence and possible fear of punishment is what you are seeing, not guilt. The puppy or dog will offer appeasement gestures, such as lip licking, lowering the head and ears, blinking, and looking away to avoid confrontation. In a study in 2017, researchers found that both signals, licking of lips and looking away, may serve as appeasement signals in dog–human communication.

After all this interesting research, we know that our dogs feel love for us and contentment living next to us as our companions. However, we need to be aware that our puppies and dogs show emotion, stress, and concern through their body language which we need to learn how to interpret and listen to.

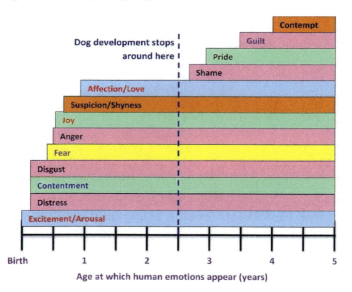

Figure 1.

References

Angelika Firnkes, Angela Bartels, Emilie Bidoli, Michael Erhard,
Appeasement signals used by dogs during dog–human communication,
Journal of Veterinary Behaviour, Volume 19, 2017, Pages 35-44, ISSN 1558-7878

Dog Enrichment & the World of Scent

Dogs possess up to 300 million olfactory receptors in their noses, compared to about six million in humans. The part of a dog's brain that is devoted to analysing smells is, proportionally speaking, 40 times greater than ours. Amazing! Our puppies and dogs really do see their world through scent.

Dog's noses also function quite differently than our own. When we inhale, we smell and breathe through the same airways within our nose. When dogs inhale, a fold of tissue just inside their nostril helps to separate these two functions.

In humans, the sense of smell is relegated to a small region on the roof of our nasal cavity, along the main airflow path. The air we smell just goes in and out with the air we breathe. In dogs, about 12 percent of the inspired air, detours into a recessed area in the back of the nose that is dedicated to olfaction, while the rest of the incoming air sweeps past that nook and disappears down through the pharynx to the lungs. Within the recessed area, the odour-laden air filters through a labyrinth of scroll-like bony structures called turbinates. Olfactory receptors within the tissue that lines the turbinates, in turn, "recognize" these odour molecules by their shape and dispatch electrical signal to the brain for analysis.

Olfactory Bulb: Part of the brain that processes signals from the olfactory epithelium. In dogs, the canine olfactory bulbs are 3 times larger than those found in humans, despite having brains that are 10 times smaller.

Olfactory Epithelium: A catacomb type structure at the back of the nasal passage that houses sensory receptors. In dogs per surface area in comparison to humans have millions of receptors more than humans.

Vomeronasal Organ: The sensory organ that detects pheromones, which are picked up by a dog's wet nose.

Nostrils: Air is exhaled through the side slits, so that scent coming in through the nose is not diluted.

When we exhale through our nose, we send the spent air out the way it came in, forcing out any incoming odours. When dogs exhale, the spent air exits through the slits in the sides of their noses. The manner in which the exhaled air swirls out actually helps usher new odours into the dog's nose. More importantly, it allows dogs to sniff continuously.

Dogs have a second olfactory capability that we don't have, made possible by an organ we don't possess: the vomeronasal organ, also known as Jacobson's organ. Located in the bottom of a dog's nasal passage, Jacobson's organ picks up pheromones, the chemicals unique to each animal species that advertise sex-related details and information. The pheromone molecules that the organ detects—and their analysis by the brain—do not get mixed up with odour molecules or their analysis, because the organ has its own nerves leading to a part of the brain devoted entirely to interpreting its signals. It's as if Jacobson's organ had its own dedicated computer server.

Now we've looked at the biology of scent for dogs we can now see how odour, scentwork, tracking, detection, scent games and puzzles are important for a dog's wellbeing and enrichment. The types of enrichment for our dogs are Social Enrichment, Physical Enrichment, Cognitive Enrichment, Sensory Enrichment, Feeding Enrichment and Toy Enrichment. Keeping your dog physically active and in shape is an important part of dog wellness, but it is also important to provide mental stimulation for your dog. Problem solving and scent-based activities like puzzle toys, snuffle mats, lickimats and kongs are a great way to provide mental stimulation to your dog both when you are with them and when you're not at home. The toys come in the form of puzzles which hide treats and encourage the dog to figure out how to move, slide, sniff and snuffle the treat hidden. Dog safe bubbles in tasty flavours, different textures and things to explore like tunnels and sand pits are all fun ways to create an interesting environment to explore.

We have to be aware not to make things too complicated too soon for the puppy or dog, as they could get frustrated if they can't figure it out quickly. Frustration often leads to stress which we want to reduce or eliminate with scent activities. 10 minutes of scentwork is equivalent stimulation as an hour's walk. This is worth thinking about for when our dogs may be injured, recovering from illness, older or for days perhaps we are unwell and cannot take our dogs for a walk. Likewise, for days following a negative experience, for example fireworks, a day of rest with scent led gentle games in the garden can help reduce the stress hormone cortisol. Our dogs like us need time to process, relax and de-stress from negative experiences and avoid trigger stacking. A trigger, in dog behaviour language, is an addition to the environment that causes a dog to increase their awareness/fear/reactivity. Anything that constitutes a stressful trigger adds another layer of stress to what a dog is experiencing.

PUPPY CLASS - A 6 WEEK SESSION PLAN

WEEK 1 – At Venue: Owners Only In Class

This will take place at the booked venue of choice without your puppy. A chance to meet Suzy, ask questions, discuss all things puppy, puppy behaviour and talk about those first days, weeks with your puppy. Plus, watch demonstrations from our demo dogs if present and learn key foundations to behaviours we will cover over the following 5 weeks. This 6 week course can be followed at home with this book and lots of yummy treats, plus the training schedules.

Behaviour Foundations we will look at if working in-person:

Capturing eye contact and check ins – Puppy offers eye contact = reward

Reflex to Name – Name = reward (Positive association to name)

Enrichment Ideas: Using cardboard boxes, flowerpots, egg boxes, toilet rolls etc., that can be used to set up "Freework" or a what we like to think as a big scenting adventure. Hide treats in all the items, different heights, rooms and in the garden then bring your dog into the room to explore.

We will also discuss:

- What is socialisation and what does it mean to our dogs?
- Fireworks and Sound Sensitivity
- Dog Body Language and Understanding Stress Signals
- Toilet Training
- Crate/Confinement Training
- Dog's and Children
- Puppy Biting
- Dog Law
- Appropriate Play, Greetings and Interaction with dogs and people
- Harness, Lead and Collar Desensitisation and Equipment
- Using a clicker and marker word

"**Freework**" and scent-based activities work well before and after a walk as a warmup and cool down, encouraging puppy or dog to seek and find scent. Offering different scent activities also offers choice to our dogs, choosing which puzzle or activity, which also builds confidence. This is something you can set up after putting on puppy or dog's harness, which will help lower arousal and any frustration prior to a walk. These activities are also useful to set up during 'puppy witching hour', when puppies become overstimulated, over tired or struggling with teething.

Following a walk, play or training session, particularly an adventurous one filled with stimulation, prep a yummy, filled Kong, a Lickimat, or have a tasty long-lasting chew ready to aid relaxation and rest.

WEEK 2

Getting Puppy Skills Started

- Teaching a Drop Cue: Teaching release of an item and adding a cue.
- Jumping Up – Keeping Paws on the Floor: reinforcing wanted behaviour to see it repeated.
- Food Manners: Teaching our dogs what behaviours we want around food.
- Settling and Capturing Calm: Capturing settling on a blanket or mat.

WEEK 3

Recall Week

- Reflex to your puppy's name: Name = Eye Contact/Check-In
- Charging the Recall Cue: Choosing a recall cue and charging it up.
- Recall Games: The Counting Game
- Hand Target: For recall, moving your dog and veterinary visits.

WEEK 4

Cues to keep your puppy safe

- Teaching a Stay/Wait: Building this behaviour and slowly increasing the 3 'D's.
- Door and Gate Safety for Dogs
- Teaching a Leave: Leave = Immediate check-in / Leave item/stimulus
- Loose Lead Foundations: Using captured eye contact and check-ins as foundations to loose lead.

WEEK 5

Husbandry and Cooperative Care Focus

- Teaching a Stand for Vet Visits
- Beginning Muzzle Training: Using scentwork and target work.
- The Bucket Game: How we use this game for cooperative care and relaxation.
- Loose Lead Skills – Follow Me Method: Building loose lead.

WEEK 6

Building Our Puppy Skills

- Practicing Recall Skills by adding distraction
- Loose Lead Walking – Using your foundation and follow me skills in practice around distraction outside.
- Recap on Cues and Behaviours.

WEEK ONE – DOG OWNERS ONLY IN CLASS

Our Week One is an introduction to our puppy course without your puppy. A chance to meet Suzy, ask questions, discuss all things puppy, puppy behaviour and talk about those first days, weeks with your puppy. We want you to feel supported, have fun in class and enjoy teaching your puppy, plus know that we are on hand with help.

Support for puppy and dog owners is as important to us, as that for your canine companions. Making the amazing decision to add a dog to you family is magical, watching them develop and grow, but also stressful from the amount of care, teaching and often lack of sleep! This is something that Suzy understands well from taking care of foster puppies and dogs.

In our puppy classes we will be covering key life skills and behaviours, looking at canine body language and behaviour, husbandry and how to support and care your puppy through training and wellness as they develop and grow.

Puppy Classes are generally run at Chipping Sodbury Grammar Rooms, beginning with Suzy meeting you at the entrance to the venue and showing you where to come with your puppies in the following weeks. Week One is without puppies, which gives us the opportunity to answer questions and talk through what the following 5 weeks will encompass. Suzy may also demo with their dogs some of the foundations to behaviours we will cover.

Puppy classes will be limited to 4-6 puppies per group maximum, along with Suzy. Puppy spaces will be marked out with cones or poles, maintaining social distance and space for each puppy to be comfortable. If puppies are a little sensitive, we will change the set up to suit each individual puppy and owner, to prevent overstimulation and maintain enjoyment of each session for you both.

We incorporate scentwork into nearly all of our training, due to its low impact, mental stimulation and using your puppy's incredible nose and brain. We recommend Nina Ottosson puzzles and games, snufflemats, slow feeders and utilizing your gardens, grass and hedges as nature's snuffling. (Note: Let your puppy pull on a toy rather than you tugging to prevent injury.)

We will also talk through basic cues such as 'Sit' and 'Down' which are often the first cues that owners will teach, and how sometimes these cues become overused and why some dogs may not be comfortable in these positions, due to the cold surfaces, pain, discomfort for example.

We will also discuss:

- What is socialisation? What does it mean to our dogs?
- Fireworks and Sound Sensitivity
- Dog Body Language and Understanding Stress Signals.
- Toilet Training
- Crate/Confinement Training
- Dog's and Children
- Puppy Biting
- Dog Law
- Appropriate Play, Greetings and Interaction with dogs and people.
- Harness, Lead and Collar Desensitisation and equipment.
- Using a clicker and marker word in training.

Safe Exercise for Puppies

Puppies require different needs, exercise, sleep and activities to an adult dog for a number of reasons. Exercise and enrichment are important for healthy bodies and enrichment; however, we are here to guide you in appropriate activities for your puppy.

Growth plates are soft, spongy areas that are located at the ends of the long bones in puppies and young dogs. They are present to be slowly filled with cells through development into adolesence, allowing your puppy's bones bones to become longer and more dense. The cells work by dividing themselves and filling the growth plate. Maturity and full growth occurs around 2 years, sometimes longer for larger breeds when growth plates close and are solid bone.

Until the growth plates close, they're soft and vulnerable to injury. (Killion, J; 2015, Puppy Culture) Dog's, like people, don't reach their

TRAINING & BONDING TIPS

Lots of high value, yummy treats are needed for this week. Hatheralls Yard has a great natural pet food store and the Mutty Professor in Bristol stocks amazing treats, chews and yummy things. We love buying dried sausage to cut up into small pieces.

For the Bucket Game you will need:

- A Small Bucket
- Treats
- Settlemat or a bed
- Safe place

maximum bone density until after puberty. The guideline for appropriate exercise is 5 Minutes/Month Age. A 12-week puppy would require 15 minutes. We also need to protect puppies from over stimulation, 'flooding' and gently introduce them to the world and appropriate dogs that can teach dog communication and acceptable play.

Dog Greetings and Socialisation

"Socialisation is the process of introducing your puppy to new experiences in a positive way, so that he learns that the world is a great big fun place. Gentle exposure to new people, places, sounds, and experiences will help build your puppy's confidence." (Schnade, V., 2009; p77)

Puppy socialisation begins from birth, learning about the sights, sounds, textures of their world and the world of humans. Puppies are able to recognise their littermates at 4 to 5 weeks and form attachments to humans and other animals during primary socialisation. Regular positive human handling of puppies during the primary period and stimulation has been shown in a study that dogs are more resilient to stress as an adult. (Howell et al, 2015) Finding a breeder that has begun careful socialisation and habituation, looking at the environment of the puppies and littermate interactions is important for choosing the right companion.

A puppy's early social contact and habituation to different stimuli, objects, loud noises such as traffic and exposure to different environments are the foundations for a dog to be able to cope with further environments as well as form bonds with humans. (Serpell & Jagoe, 1995) This introduction to the world reduces a dog perhaps becoming fearful or anxious later on.

Socialising your puppy to the world and creating positive associations to different environments and stimuli is key for your puppy to confidently live in our human world. Socialising does not just mean to other canine friends but to a car, the hoover, bikes, prams, children, traffic, different people, textures, sand, water, in fact as many experiences as possible. However, make sure that each experience is positive and at the puppy's pace and distance they are comfortable with. For example, introduce a hoover at a distance, with one person playing or sprinkling treats into a snufflemat with puppy, while another turns a hoover on and then off. This can be repeated, switching the hoover on and off. Associating the sound and movement of the hoover slowly, building up time the hoover is switched on with yummy and good things. This is part of 'desensitisation' to a new stimulus.

Socialisation is much more than socialising our puppies with other puppies and dogs. Capturing calm behaviour and interactions is more important socially than allowing dogs free play, that could lead to overstimulation and unwanted learnt behaviour. Many adult dogs are not tolerant of puppies, which could lead to negative experiences or injury. Always think quality over quantity with social experiences. Working with a rewards-based dog trainer will give you further guidance and many professionals offer guided walks, helping dog owners with positive dog-dog interactions.

Training, or rather teaching our dogs wanted behaviours and cues, is key to puppy development, using reward-based methods for husbandry and cooperative care. In the case of some dogs, coat care is additionally important, so training needs to begin from the moment the dog arrives. Grooming needs to be a positive experience, along with handling for veterinary consults to nail clipping. Some dogs we have worked with like to sit on the sofa as their nails are trimmed, as this space is comfortable.

We encourage our puppy training clients to take their puppies to cafes, charity shops for treats, Chipping Sodbury has some of the loveliest staff that welcome dogs and who have yummy treats in a jar. Different textures under their paws like sand, concrete, gravel and grass, walks past other animals, traffic. A stroll around a pet store is a fun and positive experience, from the yummy food sniffs to the meeting of other dogs and people. Take yummy treats with you, rewarding behaviour and supporting positive associations. If your puppy shows any signs of fear (lip licking, blinking, tension) or reluctance, increase your distance from the stimulus that may be a little scary. Scatter some treats into grass to allow your puppy to snuffle. This will create again a positive association with the new stimulus but is at a distance your puppy is relaxed and comfortable.

Get creative at home too! Fill a cardboard box with toys, some treats, toilet rolls etc. and encourage your puppy to explore and explode. The noises, bangs and movement is all good exposure to sound and scent. Hide treats around an area in your home or a trail in the garden and encourage your puppy to sniff and use their nose. A dog's olfactory system is incredible.

This article from the Dogs Trust has great information. Dogs Trust also have sound therapy files too.

https:///help-advice/behaviour/puppy-socialisation-introduction

https:///help-advice/dog-behaviour-health/sound-therapy-for-pets

Puppy Culture Learning

https:///pages/the-learning-center

Fireworks and Sound Sensitivity

There are lots of things we can do to help and support dogs around and before fireworks events during the year, Guy Fawkes Night, Christmas and New Year are some of those events that use fireworks in celebration however, those of us with fearful pets often dread the lead up to these calendar dates. Fireworks also impact on our wildlife, the environment, livestock, horses and more, it was significant that Sainsbury's Supermarket stopped selling the products a few years ago. We hope more retailers and supermarkets follow their lead. Always seek veterinary support if your puppy dog is experiencing behaviour changes or sensitivity. This information is to prepare for time of year that our canine companions need additional support.

Personal Experience

Currently our dogs do not exhibit large amounts of stress from fireworks. However, precautions to keep them relaxed involve early walks and toilet breaks before evening, frozen Kong's prepped to aid settling, music or a movie playing and sometimes they like a TTouch Half Wrap. Thundershirts, work well in a similar way for many dogs too from their gentle, constant pressure that can have a calming, relaxing effect. We also recommend looking at plugins from **Pet Remedy** or **Adaptil**. Pet Remedy also do a spray as well which can be sprayed on blankets, or toys that dogs can choose to be near. Prior to the fireworks events you can slowly expose your puppy/dog to fireworks/thunderstorm sounds via CD's and videos on YouTube, associating the sounds with good things. Dogs Trust have downloads to safely and gradually expose dogs to noises and a download of soothing sounds.

https://www.dogstrust.org.uk/help-advice/dog-behaviour-health/sound-therapy-for-pets

Begin exposing your puppy or dog slowly, at low volumes for short periods and slowly build. I like to use cheese and filled yummy Kong's and Lickimats during this activity as the good thing to associate with the different noises.

"Noise phobias are common in animals. Some examples of fear-evoking noise stimuli are thunder, gunshots, and fireworks." (Landsberg. G, 2008; p251)

Our previous dog, Jack, a West Highland Terrier was terrified of Fireworks and Storms. With any dog exhibiting fearful behaviour please consult your vet in regard to possible medication and a behaviourist or rewards-based trainer for advice in the lead up to fireworks and to build a plan. Jack would cry, shake, toilet in the home and the stress would affect him for days. We had vet support, but also created a safe place for him in an area he chose with blankets, held and comforted him, closed curtains and placed cushions around for him to hide and rest. Encouraging Jack to his safe place to hide helped him stop pacing and shaking.

In a study from 2015 that looked at fear sensitivity in different dog breeds, 23% of the dogs were reported to be fearful of noises, which is a little more than one out of every five dogs. The study looked at 17 different breeds and confirmed that some breeds and likewise the gender of the dog, (female dogs were found to be 30% more likely to show fear), were significantly more fearful of loud sounds, showing that there is a genetic predisposition to sensitivity. Other factors were noted within the study and in conclusion showed that behaviour may be the result of heredity and physiology, rather than just a stressful event.

How can we help support our dogs?

- Speak to your dog's vet about further support, supplements such as YuCalm, Dorwest herbal support, Nutracalm and veterinary medication.

- Contact a qualified behaviourist or certified trainer for ongoing training. Look at the ABTC, APBC, ICAN, APDT, INTODogs, IMDT etc.

- **Fear is an emotion, not a behaviour** which means it cannot be reinforced by operant conditioning. Comforting and reassuring your dog will not reinforce fear. Fear is an emotion; the fear response begins in the amygdala. A threat stimulus, in this case fireworks triggers a fear response in the amygdala, which activates areas with the dog related to motor functions involved in fight or flight. It also triggers a release of stress hormones and the sympathetic nervous system. So, make sure your dog is also secure within your home/garden preventing potential escape from fear flight. Make sure your pets microchip, tag details are up to date and fences are secure.

- If your puppy/dog takes treats during fireworks, prepare some yummy goodies and sprinkle treats when fireworks are heard. You could use a snufflemat or a Lickmat for extra sniffing and licking. Make up some yummy Kongs and have some long-lasting treats in the cupboard.

- Cortisol, the stress hormone takes at least 72 hours to leave the system, sometimes following a fearful event can take weeks for your dog to recover. Bear this in mind after your dog has had a stressful event, or after an evening post fireworks. Your dog may need a quiet day at home with sniffy games, long lasting treats or a quiet scent led walk. Missing walks allowing cortisol to leave your dog's body is recommended. This will also help avoid trigger stacking. (Trigger Stacking is where a number of events occur before your dog has had time to process, and their stress signals have not returned to normal.)

Figure 2.

- Avoid walking your dog in the dark, even though your dog may not show any signs they are scared of fireworks, a dog can become fearful of a stimulus, particularly if the incident is very aversive, scary to them. Go outside with your dog for their last toilet trip early evening. Walk your dog earlier in the day and plan canine enrichment activities for later.

- Play music, white noise on YouTube, a film that will help soften the sounds of fireworks. Classic FM often broadcasts music for pets and owners during the Guy Fawkes Night period on and around the 5th November to help support your dog. You can purchase ear defenders for dogs, though these will require training to desensitise your dog to wearing comfortably. (I advise contacting a rewards-based trainer to help with husbandry).

- Allow your dog to choose a safe place, perhaps under a table, behind the sofa, under your bed or in a specific room for example. Add to this area placing their bed, soft blankets, placing blanket over these areas to reduce light and sound. Place some yummy treats and chews in the area to help them feel comfortable. Close curtains, blinds and windows to reduce noise and muffle fireworks sounds as much as possible.

- **Lastly, most importantly don't leave your dogs and pets alone, reassure and comfort them. You cannot reinforce fear. But your support will help soothe and reassure your dogs.**

References:

Storengen, L.M., Lingaas, F. Noise sensitivity in 17 dog breeds: prevalence, breed risk and correlation with fear in other situations. Applied Animal Behaviour Science, 2015

Emily J. Blackwell, John W. S. Bradshaw, Rachel A. Casey, Fear responses to noises in domestic dogs: Prevalence, risk factors and co-occurrence with other fear related behaviour, Applied Animal Behaviour Science, Volume 145. Issues 1–2, April 2013, Pages 15-25, 2013

Landsberg. G, Hunthausen. W, Ackerman. L, Handbook of Behaviour Problems of the Dog and Cat, 2008

Nancy A. Dreschel, Douglas A. Granger Physiological and behavioural reactivity to stress in thunderstorm-phobic dogs and their caregivers, Applied Animal Behaviour Science,

Volume 95. Issues 3-4, December 2005, Pages 153-168, 2005

PUPPY AND DOG BEHAVIOUR

The social behaviour and cognitive skills of dogs are rooted in their heritage from their wild ancestors, but these behaviours and skills were formed more or less to comply with their new (social) environment, that of humans. (Pongracz, P., 2014; p250)

Learning your dog's language will help you understand and communicate better with your puppy during their development. Learning about these subtle signs of communication is key to understanding how our puppy's and dogs are feeling.

It can be hard to decipher whether your puppy or dog is exhibiting signs of stress or anxiety, especially if you've adopted an adult or senior dog or welcomed a new puppy into your home. With any new behaviour, we recommend making notes of times of day and context which you can discuss with us by email, message or at the time of your class. Some stress signs are very subtle and can easily go unnoticed or misinterpreted. So, we recommend starting to observe your canine companion and look for body language.

Trigger Stacking is where a number of events occur before your dog has had time to process, and their stress signals have not returned to normal. One event occurring and the rest of the walk stress free, will result in a relaxed dog on return. If your dog however experiences a number of stressful events, this can then lead to what we term as 'trigger stacked.'

A few signs of stress are; yawning, tongue flicks, dry panting, frantic sniffing, refusing to go forward. (Stewart. G., 2016; p74-76) Tail wagging is often misinterpreted; however, position and motion tells us a lot about how a dog is feeling so try to observe and make notes re position and movement which you can then interpret into body language. A relaxed tail will be loose and gently wag, whereas a stiff or frantic wagging tail may show the dog is over aroused, a tucked tail may mean your dog is fearful.

Dogs can be social animals, so communication is key in maintaining a peaceful coexistence with others. Most of dog communication occurs silently through body language. Other language may be louder (barks, whines, growls, yelps, howls and so on) and seem more familiar to our human perception of language. It is likely that before a dog starts to communicate more loudly through sound, there has been some silent body language that has gone unnoticed. Scent could also play a factor in communication; dogs have a phenomenal sense of smell – something we as humans may find difficult to understand fully, as our noses are not as good.

Body Language and Trigger Stacking

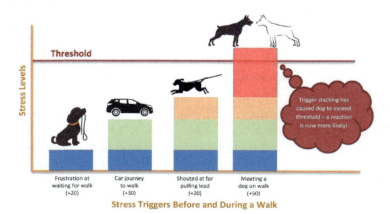

Figure 3.

SOCIALISATION AND DOG BODY LANGUAGE

Stress Signals and Signs

Stress signals such as lip licking, whale eye; whereby the whites of a dog's eyes are shown, turning away, crouched, stiff body language, ears back and yawning need to be observed and action such as increasing distance from something scary or worrying your puppy or dog may need to occur. "Shaking it off" behaviour is commonly seen in dogs and noted by owners. In the 'Dog Field Study' this behaviour was associated with a decline in pulse rates. In the study it was shown that when the dogs showed this behaviour their pulse rate was particularly high, lowering after they shook. It also showed that when dogs were sniffing in the environment their pulse rate declined as well. It was found that dogs on longer leads spent 3 times more sniffing. We encourage all our clients to carry a longer lead as well on walks, to encourage sniffing behaviour, which is good for our dogs well-being and health.

Pic 1. Lip Licking   Pic 2. Whale Eye.   Pic 3. Turning away.

Socialising Your Puppy to the World

Socialising your puppy to the world and creating positive associations to different environments and stimuli is key for your puppy to confidently live in our human world. Socialising does not just mean to other canine friends but to a car, the hoover, bikes, prams, children, traffic, different people, textures, sand, water, in fact as many experiences as possible. However, make sure that each experience is positive and at the puppy's pace and distance they are comfortable with. For example, introduce a hoover at a distance, with one person playing or sprinkling treats into a snufflemat with your puppy, while another turns a hoover on and then off. This can be repeated, switching the hoover on and off.

Associating the sound and movement of the hoover slowly, building up time the hoover is switched on with yummy and good things. This is part of 'desensitisation' to a new stimulus.

We always recommend, sniffy slow walks on different surfaces, different dogs, people, visitors, traffic, roads, cafes, pet stores, car journeys, charity shops, busy town centre and countryside along the river. Use lots of rewards to create positive associations with everything new. As adolescence approaches there are hormonal changes that occur, this can cause a sensitive fear period that is called the secondary fear period in developing puppies. This is normal and part of natural development. Do reassure your puppy if they show any concerns over any stimuli and do not force them to approach fearful objects or environments. Instead move away to a comfortable distance where puppy is relaxed and pair what makes them nervous with something he enjoys, like food.

Puppy Play/Dog Intros: You can also create positive associations with seeing dogs at different distances with yummy treats. Dog appears in the environment = reward.

Keep introductions brief and observe body language, look for relaxed body language, mirroring, play bows and balanced play. If play begins to become too much, or you are seeing bullying behaviour, recall away, lots of treats and allow your puppy some time to sniff and process. Think quality over quantity with dog meets. Consent test during puppy/dog play.

At Puppy Classes Weekly: Well managed puppy-puppy greetings.

Appropriate dog greetings with people and dogs is important to teach our companions. Meets with happy greeting, calm older dogs, that are able to teach clear body language and further communication. As puppies have soft growth plates play requires care and **'consent testing'**. (One dog is held gently by the harness, to see if the other willingly return to play)

Each week we look at safe and calm puppy-puppy meets to build confidence and reinforce wanted social behaviour. This is managed using barriers, observing and noting body language to allow less confident puppies choices and to capture calm behaviour of more confident puppies.

Multidog/Pet Households: Although dogs and cats if introduced carefully and slowly can get on well, likewise introducing a puppy or dog to other resident dogs. A slow and gentle introduction is far safer than a rushed one and will result in both animals becoming good friends. Introducing your new puppy into a different environment with other resident animals can be stressful for the puppy and likewise, often for older resident dogs.

You will need to prepare everything prior to your puppy's arrival, this will give your resident dogs time to adjust to the changes, new puppy pen and area, bed, bowls, blankets etc. Separate areas for your older dog/dogs to allow for time apart from your new puppy is key, especially in the early days while they're getting used to each other. This is equally important for important rest and sleep that both puppies and adult dogs require.

New puppy's often change the older dog's routine which can cause stress, so try to minimize this as much as possible with keeping as close to your older dog's schedule as possible. Until you are sure of how your puppy behaves being left alone with older resident dogs keep your puppy in a separate safe space, such as a puppy pen with their bed, appropriate toys and water. Setting up a camera to observe these times will help you assess how settled your dogs are when left.

Puppy pens and puppy safe areas need to be carefully introduced, creating a safe and positive place the puppy feels confident in and where they can rest. This area will also mean that your puppy does not disturb your older dog while not present that could cause conflict but also that your puppy is safe from harm too.

Puppy settling on a cool mat.　　　　　　　　　Puppy in a safe puppy pen.

Introducing your puppy is best in a more neutral area, like a front garden, courtyard, where the dogs can part and encouraged to sniff and where calm interactions can be reinforced with rewards. Setting up dog-puppy introductions for success. Many older dogs are not tolerant of puppies so careful management, observation and intervention is important by the dog owners. Puppies are easily injured by over enthusiastic play, likewise senior/disabled dogs by an adolescent puppy.

Create separate feeding areas/stations to reduce potential conflict and stress around food. This could be a mat in different rooms, supervising chews and long-lasting treats in the same way. Remove food bowls/snufflemats/slow feeders once your dogs have finished eating.

Children and Your Puppy

Introducing your puppy to children carefully is important to keep both children and your puppy safe. Most importantly, no hugging or picking up the puppy, both of which can cause your puppy stress and often discomfort. This is where we may hear a growl or possibly see a bite from the puppy feeling uncomfortable or possibly threatened.

As we have discussed in the puppy pack, sleep and rest is important for healthy puppy development, so we need to make children aware not to disturb a puppy when resting. A puppy or dog can also become easily startled if disturbed and children need to be aware that puppies and dogs need rest.

Puppies are often over excited, so teaching children appropriate play and interaction is key. Don't have children offering their hand towards a puppy or dog to sniff, this action can often be interpreted by dogs as a threat and potentially result in a bite. Instead encourage calm activities, like setting up some scent games, or involving them during training sessions. Puppy biting can often be a problem, so having an adult always present with children is important to prevent accidents and intervene when energy increases. Discourage and stop chasing games, these can lead to overstimulation and a growing puppy can easily knock over a small child.

Equally important is teaching your children about swapping and exchanging items with your puppy or dog, building trust and reducing stress and potential accidents. Teaching our children how our puppies and dogs learn, using positive reinforcement will create a great relationship.

Preparation really is the key when you are expecting a baby. Consider thinking about your relationship with your dog and what they are like around children. Sometimes we do not know about our dog's responses around babies, so we need to have these considerations. If you have friends with babies or small children, perhaps ask if your puppy, dog can meet them safely on lead in a controlled environment, creating positive associations using treats and rewards. We advise speaking to a professional about desensitising and preparations for a baby.

Behaviour around Food: To build our puppy's and dog's confidence of us and children around their food/chews/toys never take food or items from your puppy or dog. Place the dog's meal down in a quiet space for them to eat. Drop food into the puppy's bowl or snufflemat and have children do the same as they walk past at a distance. **Your presence = Food and good things.**

The same goes for chews/toys/items, remember to trade for a treat. This can be built into swapping with your puppy or dog. Trade a toy for a few treats sprinkled on the floor, pick up the toy, when your puppy has finished eating their treats, offer the toy back to them. This will build trust around people picking up toys and items and decrease potential frustration, which can escalate to resource guarding and dogs ingesting items.

Overstimulation: Dogs can experience overstimulation when overtired, frustrated, or experiencing sensory overload. If you find your puppy is overstimulated on a walk, perhaps chewing the lead, pulling, stressed, then change the environment, move away from what is perhaps an environment with too much happening for e.g., a busy road with noisy traffic. Engage your dog into some nice sniffy games in a quieter space. Do not be afraid to cut a walk short and head home for rest, sensory games and training.

Desensitisation is the process of exposing an animal to a stimulus beginning at a very low intensity. Gradually exposing to the new/fearful stimulus, starting at a very low level and building up very slowly. It should be systematic, which means we have to create a plan to build up gradually. Every time we change the level as we progress, your dog needs to be happy and comfortable. Hence, we have to note body language and stress signs.

If we notice your dog is even a little fearful or scared, we need to immediately return back to an easier stage of the plan and go back a few steps. If we move ahead too fast and frighten your dog, then we could instead be doing sensitisation (making the problem worse) rather than **systematic desensitisation**. These steps are to be done at your puppy/dog's pace.

New Sounds: The Hoover Example

In the same way we can desensitise to new stimuli, I am going to use the hoover as an example of how to slowly introduce a new sound and create a positive association.

The hoover needs to be introduced slowly, without sound or movement as we pair with treats or a Lickimat. Hoover = Treat scatter, dropped to snuffle.

Turn the hoover on briefly for 2 seconds, at a distance your dog is comfortable with and then off, while dropping treats for your dog to snuffle. A snufflemat would be great for this exercise.

Once your dog is comfortable with the sight and sound for 2 seconds, build to 3, 4, 5 seconds and so on. Continue dropping treats or prepare a Lickimat ready for this exercise.

Add in movement gently of the hoover, turn on for 2 seconds, then like before increase the time slowly.

Introduce this activity into different rooms, slowly building, increasing duration the hoover is switched on and movement. If your dog shows any stress signals, such as lip licking, blinking, low tail, stop, go back a few steps. We are slowly developing a positive association with the hoover.

Flooding: This means prolonged exposure to a stimulus until the puppy/dog eventually stops reacting. This is the opposite of the approach taken in desensitisation (exposing a dog slowly to a stimulus at a low level/distance). It causes increased stress (cortisol) and will cause further behaviour problems and an animal to shut down (Seligman. M. 1972). The most common problem is increased fear.

Therefore, up-to-date dog trainers encourage puppy owners to be careful during sensitive periods of development, introducing puppies slowly to new stimuli and new environments. This includes awareness of which dogs you socialise your puppy with, many adult dogs are not tolerant of young, rude and often bouncy puppies jumping on them and in their face. If this behaviour is not intervened by the owners and left, this can lead to an older dog reacting with aggressive behaviour, which could become a negative learning experience for the puppy. Likewise, for the adult dog, as felt they had to escalate to stop the puppies unwanted advances and interaction. Always ask the other owners permission for your dog to meet the other to prevent potential conflict. Watch body language closely and separate before escalation.

Dogs and the Law

Controlling Dogs in Public

https://www.gov.uk/control-dog-public

It's against the law to let a dog be dangerously out of control anywhere, such as:

- in a public place
- in a private place, for example a neighbour's house or garden
- in the owner's home

The law applies to all dogs.

Out of control

Your dog is considered dangerously out of control if it:

- injures someone
- makes someone worried that it might injure them

A court could also decide that your dog is dangerously out of control if either of the following apply:

- it attacks someone's animal
- the owner of an animal thinks they could be injured if they tried to stop your dog attacking their animal

A farmer is allowed to kill your dog if it's worrying their livestock.

Public Spaces Protection Orders

Some public areas in England and Wales are covered by Public Spaces Protection Orders (PSPOs) - previously called Dog Control Orders (DCOs).

In public areas with PSPOs, you may have to:

- keep your dog on a lead
- put your dog on a lead if told to by a police officer, police community support officer or someone from the council
- stop your dog going to certain places - like farmland or parts of a park
- limit the number of dogs you have with you (this applies to professional dog walkers too)
- clear up after your dog
- carry a poop scoop and disposable bags

BSL: Banned dogs

In the UK, it's against the law to own certain types of dog. These are the:

- Pit Bull Terrier
- Japanese Tosa
- Dogo Argentino
- Fila Brasileiro

It's also against the law to:

- sell a banned dog
- abandon a banned dog
- give away a banned dog
- breed from a banned dog

Whether your dog is a banned type depends on what it looks like, rather than its breed or name.

Identification

Collar and tag

The law (Control of Dogs Order 1992) states that your dog must wear a collar and a tag when in public. The tag must have your name and address on; your telephone number can be helpful too. Without a collar it is possible that your dog may be seized and treated as a stray. You should always keep the contact details on the tag up-to-date.

Microchip

From 2015 in Wales and 2016 in England the law has made it compulsory for owners to have their dogs microchipped (if they are over 8 weeks of age). At the RSPCA they microchip all their dogs before they are rehomed but under law the owner is responsible for keeping the contact details up-to-date and failure to do so can result in a fine. That means if you move home or change your phone number you need to update the details.

Stray dogs

Having a collar and tag are essential in case he/she goes missing. Should your dog go missing your local authority should be your first point of contact. They have the responsibility for strays and may charge you a fee to reclaim your dog. If a dog is not claimed within 7 days, the local authority has the right to rehome or euthanise the dog. Up -to-date identification will make it easier for your dog to be reunited with you.

Microchipping

https://www.gov.uk/get-your-dog-microchipped

You must make sure your dog is fitted with a microchip by the time it's 8 weeks old.

Your dog's microchip must be fitted by a trained professional, for example a vet.

You can ask the following to microchip your dog for free:

- Battersea Dogs and Cats Home
- Blue Cross centres
- Dogs Trust

You can also ask your vet or local council if they can microchip your dog. They might charge a fee.

You're responsible for keeping your dog's microchip information up to date, for example if you move house.

Contact the database company your dog is registered with to update any of your details.

If you do not have the microchip number, you can ask any of the following to scan your dog for it:

- a vet
- a dog warden
- a dog rescue centre

Control of dogs

https://www.legislation.gov.uk/ukpga/1991/65/contents

Dangerously out of control dogs

It is a criminal offence (Dangerous Dog Act 1991) to allow your dog to be 'dangerously out of control' either in a public place or on private property e.g. your home. A 'dangerously out of control' dog can be defined as a dog that has injured someone or a dog that a person has grounds to reasonably believe that it may injure somebody. Something as simple as your dog chasing, barking at or jumping up at a person or child could result in an investigation, so ensure your dog is under control at all times. If your dog injures somebody, it may be seized and if convicted you could face a lengthy prison sentence and/or a fine. Your dog could also be euthanised (unless you can persuade the Courts that it is not a danger to the public, in which case it may be subject to a control order). Under the same law it is also a criminal offence if your dog attacks an assistance dog. If at any point you are concerned about your dog's behaviour or need advice on training, please get in touch with the RSPCA centre or branch where you adopted your dog from.

Livestock worrying

Dogs must never worry livestock the owner or whoever is responsible for the dog at the time will be committing an offence if the dog chases, attacks or causes suffering to livestock. A police officer may seize a dog suspected to be worrying livestock and if convicted of an offence under this Act then a person may be liable to a maximum fine of £1,000. It should be noted that a farmer may be able to shoot any dog worrying livestock if there are no other reasonable means for stopping the dog from doing this. To avoid this, keep your dog on a lead at all times when livestock are around.

Local Dog Information (Yate and Sodbury)

If you have found a lost dog or need to share information regarding a lost or found dog below are local lost and found FB groups:

https://www.facebook.com/Lost-and-Found-pets-in-BristolSouth-Glos-405753402900619/

https://www.facebook.com/groups/lostfoundstolepetsbristolandsouthglos/?ref=share

https://www.facebook.com/groups/818819064868891/?ref=share

https://www.facebook.com/groups/228409233877408/?ref=share

Dog Warden:

Please contact the dog warden in regard to lost and found pets, dog conflict and other dog related issues for advice:

https://www.southglos.gov.uk/com.../dog-control/dog-wardens/

Contact the Bristol City dog wardens on:

0117 9222500

Contact the South Gloucestershire dog wardens on:

01454 868000

Please also take a lost and found, or deceased found dog to the nearest vets during opening hours if possible, for a microchip scan. You can contact the dog warden for advice in regard to any dog related issues.

Police:

Contact the police in regard to serious dog issues and for further advice if you need help.

https://www.avonandsomerset.police.uk/.../chipping.../

DogLost:

DogLost is run by volunteers, supporting dog owners find and search for lost dogs.

https://www.facebook.com/DogLostUk/

https://www.facebook.com/groups/725949567485714/?ref=share

https://www.facebook.com/groups/doglostsouthwest/?ref=share

Harness, Lead and Collar Desensitisation

Walking a dog with a comfortable well fit walking harness is safer and more comfortable than walking a dog with a traditional collar. Protecting the soft neck tissue and trachea from damage, should your dog pull, lunge or jump. However, many dog are afraid and apprehensive of their collar and the harness when placed over their heads. Introducing your puppy or dog slowly and carefully to wearing a collar, harness and lead and by creating a positive association with the equipment will mean you can get ready for a walk without over excitement or stress.

This same protocol can be used for a collar, slowly placing the collar over your dogs neck, feeding yummy treats and then building to desensitising to the sound of the clip when being done up.

- **Step 1:** Place the harness flat on the floor and sprinkle some yummy treats around it so your puppy or dog can investigate, sniff and start to associate it with good things. Slowly, move the harness, desensitising your dog to the sound and movement of the harness near them and continue to sprinkle treats.

    Harness = Good things/yummy treats.

- **Step 2:** Lift up the harness and feed your dog some of their favourite treats through the head-hole, placing your hand all the way through so your dog doesn't have to put their head through at this early stage. Make it as easy as possible so your dog feels happy and comfortable having their head near the harness.
- **Step 3:** You can now start to move your hand backwards away from the head-hole, luring your dog with a treat in your hand, so that your dog has to move their nose and muzzle through the harness loop in order to have the reward. If your dog shows any signs of concern, you can continue to use treats to lure them through slowly until they volunteer the movement forward.
- **Step 4:** Once your puppy or dog is comfortable with the harness being moved over their head you can move on to letting the harness hang gently around their neck while you continue to feed them treats. If they retreat and move away, simply remove the harness immediately and go back a step. Building steps slowly to create a positive association and no stress.
- **Step 5:** Desensitise clip/buckle sounds. We need to make sure your dog is comfortable with the noise of the clips first by simply clipping the harness up while you're holding it, so they can hear the sound at a small distance. As you clip together, sprinkle treats, this will pair the sound with yummy things. When your puppy or dog is comfortable with the sounds, then place the harness over their head and reward, sprinkle treats on the floor, and then do up the clips around their body. Giving them tasty treats again straight afterwards will mean they will associate having their harness done up with good things happening.
- **Step 6:** Removing the harness. Sprinkle treats on the floor and unclip the fastenings, drop treats again if your dog is perhaps moving away from you. Hold a treat and gently begin to remove the harness over your dog's head, release the treat from your hand and move the harness over your dog's head.

- **Step 7:** Once your dog has their harness on, get them used to wearing it while they move about by encouraging them into activity, such as playing a game with their favourite toy, practising training cues or a treat search. Once your dog is comfortable wearing the harness, drop treats and clip the lead onto the harness. Sprinkle a few more treats and unclip.
- **Step 8:** Once your dog is comfortable with the lead being clipped on, let the lead trail behind them, so that they can get used to feeling of the lead around their body and trailing for if you use a longline. (Longlines should always be used on a harness only to prevent neck and throat injuries.) Continue to reward and feed your dog and sprinkle treats.

Charging up your Clicker/Marker Word

We use a clicker or marker word during training to help a dog recognise when they've carried out a wanted behaviour that will lead to a reward.

Clickers used in training can be bought online or in most pet shops, though you can use a unique noise (or a specific visual signal for deaf animals), or marker word that won't be used outside of a training context.

If your dog is noise sensitive and the clicker sound is worrying them, you can muffle the sound by clicking the clicker from inside your pocket, some clickers have a soft sound as well. If they are still scared of the sound, then use a marker word instead.

Clicker training works because your dog learns to associate one thing (the click) with another (the reward such as a food treat). The clicker becomes paired with the reward. A click is always followed by a reward at first to help your dog understand it's a good thing. Once you can see that your dog is anticipating the food when they hear the click, you can start introducing the clicker to mark wanted behaviour.

Before you start using a clicker, you will need to associate the 'click' with something positive, the reward. This teaches your dog to anticipate their treat after they hear the 'click'.

Shaping

Clicker training is a useful way to get a dog to work out what you want them to do of their own accord. This uses their clever brain and is a great way to mentally stimulate them.

Shaping is the process by which you can gradually teach your dog a new behavior by rewarding them during each step of the process while learning that behavior. Breaking up more complicated actions into gradual, smaller steps so that your dog will learn and understand. Small successes will also decrease potential frustration in training.

To use the clicker, first decide what the final behaviour is that you would like your dog to do, and then break it down into small steps. These should be progressive steps that if all clicked, rewarded and built on in sequence will eventually get you to the final behaviour.

The Clicker(click)/Marker Word(good/yes) (Secondary Reinforcer) = Reward/Treat (Primary Reinforcer).

The clicker or marker word will help reinforce and capture a wanted behaviour.

- Clicker training involves two kinds of conditioning. Firstly, 'classical conditioning' (Pavlov) in which association is made where a stimulus acquires the capacity to evoke a response that was originally evoked by another stimulus. Pairing the click with a treat, therefore, initially simultaneously and then sometimes with an occasional delay, click-then-treat, creates this, Pavlovian conditioning, plus some tolerance for a slightly delayed treat.

- Practice daily with 20 repetitions to charge the Clicker or Marker Word.

- Click immediately at the behaviour you want and follow with a reward. We click and treat during a wanted behaviour, several times in rapid succession to reinforce. Immediately we are adding in the 'operant conditioning', using the clicker to mark a specific behaviour as it is happening, capturing it.

- Secondly, Operant Conditioning is where we add or remove a reward or aversive stimulus to modify behaviour. As force free positive reinforcement trainers, we add rewards to reinforce a behaviour.

- Practice Clicker Timing. Repetition is key but keep training to 5 minutes at a time. 30-50 repetitions will teach a new cue or behaviour, but keep the training periods short, with fun free play, like tuggy afterwards.

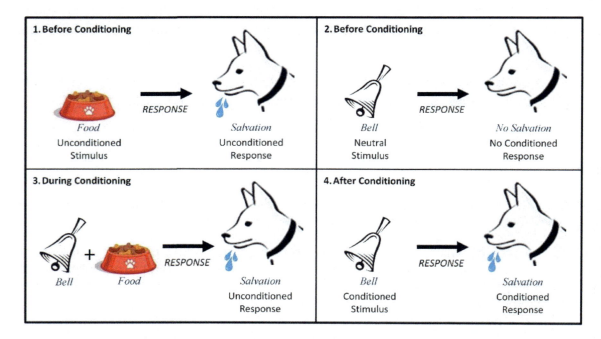

Figure 4. **Classical Conditioning (Pavlov)**

You can also add a *release cue* like, 'Free'. Throw a treat away from you or to the side of you as you say your release cue. This is a good way for your dog to know that the training session has stopped or ended. Throw treat away + Cue the word "Free" (chosen release word)

Photo: Marking eye contact/ focus using a clicker.

Crate/ Confinement Training and Settling

Crate Training has many useful real-life reasons to desensitise our dogs to confinement. Firstly, vet visits and stays, if a dog is crate trained and habituated to a crate their vet stay will be more relaxed and less stressful for your companion. Another use of confinement is in a car for safety. It is also important to start confinement training at home slowly, since confinement will be necessary during transportation, car rides can be stressful and cause motion sickness due to dog seat belt, car crates or boot space. Desensitising your puppy or dog to this safely at home and then introducing crate/settle training in the car will be helpful in creating a positive association to your vehicle.

Desensitising

Desensitisation is a behaviour modification technique and a form of classical conditioning. It works by exposing your dog to a new or triggering stimulus slowly, whereby the dog is not stressed, thereby setting the dog up to not respond (or desensitise) to the stimulus. (Serpell. J, 2018) This helps change the response to a stimulus, in this case creating a positive association with the crate and a safe place for a puppy or dog to choose to go to relax and rest. Having a crate or settle area allows a dog to have much needed rest (a puppy requires 18-20 hours sleep), process new information and regulate emotions.

Setting up the Crate

Have the crate open, with soft, clean bedding arranged, crate clipped water bowl, (Dogs need access to water at all times) and perhaps a few favourite toys. Throw some yummy treats inside the crate and let your puppy or dog investigate. Continue doing this, allowing your dog to choose to stay or leave the crate. Slowly, build to reinforcing that when your dog chooses to settle in the crate, lots of yummy treats are given. As your dog settles for longer periods and relaxed perhaps try a longer lasting treats like a yummy, filled Kong.

Once your puppy or dog is laying, settling and relaxed, captured by your yummy treats, reinforcing that the crate is safe and means good things, close the door for a few seconds, open and reward. Build this up very slowly. With any signs of distress, open the crate, toss some treats into the space and start training again another time. Build up duration, until your dog is happy and relaxed while you make a cup of tea and then open the crate door. Your dog may choose to stay in the space, snuggled with a Kong. Slowly building the time you close the crate door will create a positive association. This same method can be used for a car crate.

Puppy Biting and Chewing

Puppies learn Bite Inhibition from their mother and siblings during early development and can teeth up to 12 months of age. Often puppies that leave their litter early have not been taught these valuable lessons. It is important to remember that puppies will be experiencing some discomfort during teething periods in the same way that children do, so make sure that you give them lots of opportunities to relieve this by providing age-appropriate chews and toys.

Puppies investigate the world using their mouths so it's perfectly natural to expect them to nibble and investigate they are young. Puppies also need to use their mouths and teeth a great deal to find out how this important part of their anatomy works. Puppies will typically attempt to play with humans by mouthing and play biting. It is something that they did in the litter with their siblings (and usually mum) and it's a very normal part of learning how to play with dogs. However, we are often left to teach a puppy that biting people isn't a behaviour we want. This is taught by reinforcing calm behaviour and offering age-appropriate toys, tuggys, chews and treats to help puppies during teething and dogs when over stimulated.

Mouthing and chewing are normal dog behaviours. So, we need to give our dogs plenty of opportunities to do this in a safe and acceptable way, redirecting mouthing and chewing into appropriate play. If your puppy experiences the 'puppy witching' hour in the evening, this may be due to overstimulation or tiredness, so think about giving your puppy a long-lasting chew, filled Kong or a sniffy game or activity.

What to Avoid

- Don't encourage play biting with fingers, we especially need to be careful around children. We do not want your puppy growing up to learn that play biting is an appropriate way of interacting with people.

- Avoid using high-pitched squealing or similar noises in an attempt to let your puppy know they have hurt you. This will overexcite your puppy which often encourages more biting behaviour.
- Do not tell your dog off. Understandably puppy play bites are painful, but you don't want to frighten them as they may begin to lose trust in you or become fearful. It's better to expect and anticipate mouthing episodes, and then manage them in a safe way.

Helpful Suggestions and Tips

- **Filled Kong/Lickimat:** Frozen filled Kong's filled with Primula squeezy cheese is tasty and cold on the gums. This will also act as a natural calming tool as licking helps soothe a dog. (Great for times of stress for e.g., Fireworks/moving to a new house/new baby/building work.) Make sure your Kong is age appropriate for your puppy/dog. Blueberries, bananas, natural yoghurt are a few ideas.
- **Rope Tuggy Toys:** dipped in water or chicken broth then frozen is a great way to cool sore gums and provide a fun interesting game.
- **Natural Treats:** We recommend 'Bristol Natural Pet Foods' in Hatheralls Yard, Chipping Sodbury, where you can find nutritious and tasty chews and snacks for your dog.
- **Frozen Carrots.**
- **Puppies will have their full set of teeth from 7-12 months.** Any concerns re their bite or teeth, excessive chewing or teething we recommend a visit to your dog's vet.
- **Additional Calming: Pet Remedy** plug ins and sprays, plus many other natural remedies are available for your pet.
- The 'Mutty Professor', Bristol, stocks a great range of chews and good toys for chewing too.
- **Scentwork:** Sniffy walks with a treat bag of yummy treats and cheese, using hedgerows and grass to sprinkle treats and trees to stuff things in and to sniff and find. Great for shorter walks packed with smells and stimulation to stimulate a dog's clever busy mind.
- **Sniffy Explosion:** A cardboard box filled with paper packing, toilet rolls, treats and toys, is a fun game to explode and explore in the garden or home. Or a place plastic balls into a tub and hide treats or your dog's kibble amongst the balls.
- **Chews:** Chew Roots/Buffalo Horns/Halved Antlers. Check all chews are age/size appropriate for teeth. There are many online stockists for these chews. When our dogs are bored of a chew root, we rub pure virgin coconut oil into the woody root and suddenly our dogs love it again like new!
- **Advice:** Always check with your puppy or dog's vet for any dietary concerns, changes, questions or advice. Vet practices will have a vet or vet nurse that specialises in nutrition or can refer you.

Puppy Nutrition and Food

There are many brands and types of dog food on the market that it may be difficult to know what is best to feed your puppy or dog. These include dry complete diets (kibble), wet food with or without biscuit mixer, and many more options. Good commercial complete foods should provide all the essential nutrients for your dog. We recommend visiting this website to look at food and nutrition contents.

https://www.allaboutdogfood.co.uk/

Most foods are now available to suit the different life stages: puppy, adult and senior. These have been formulated carefully to match the needs of your dog. Ensure you buy the correct one and make the transition to the next food gradually when required. A puppy should move on to adult food when it has stopped growing which is typically around 12-18 months, but this can be up to two years for large breeds. Do be guided by your food manufacturer and vet as to the exact timing of this.

Consistency with the type of food given is important so as not to cause an upset stomach. If you want to or need to introduce a new diet this should be done over the course of a few days to a week, starting with replacing only a small amount of the current food with the new food, and gradually increasing the proportion of the new food.

Guidelines on how much to feed your dog should be written on the food packet. These are guidelines only and you may need to adjust accordingly for your dog's individual needs which will be affected by their activity levels and metabolism. You will need to monitor their weight and body condition. Consult your vet for advice if you are unsure on how much to feed. It is not recommended to leave food out all day. Any uneaten food should be removed after about 20 minutes to ensure the food remains palatable and encourage good eating behaviours.

The Garden

Some plants are perfectly safe for pets, while others may just cause a mild upset tummy. Many, however, can be highly toxic or even life threatening, for example, daffodils, irises, and hyacinths. It's also important to know the symptoms of plant poisoning, so you can recognise when there is a problem and get help as soon as possible. Look for low energy, diarrhea, vomiting, blood in stools, pale gums, difficulty breathing, drooling, lack of appetite, drinking or urinating more. Look for these and immediately call your vet for advice.

Dangerous and unsuitable foods

There are a number of foods that we enjoy which can often be tempting to give to dogs, but some of these can cause digestive problems or be fatal. Consult your vet immediately if your dog eats or ingests anything of concern. Here is a list of some foods you should not feed your dog:

- Chocolate
- Caffeine
- Grapes and raisins
- Onions and garlic
- Alcohol
- Macadamia nuts
- Food containing xylitol - an artificial sweetener

Coprophagia in puppies and dogs

Coprophagia is when dogs eat their own faeces, either their own or that of another animal. It is a common problem in some puppies, which usually clears up by adulthood with good nutrition, supervision, and vet support. With puppies it often begins was littermates and exploration, then opportunistic, but they can grow out of it as they get older. However, some dogs will still try to sniff out and eat horse manure, cow dung and rabbit droppings on a walk. Dogs are facultative carnivores and do scavenge, some faeces may contain some nutritional value such as undigested fat and protein. But we still do not fully know why the behaviour occurs. It is possible that there is an emotional reason for this behaviour, for example stress related. Another reason may be a medical problem and should be treated to try and identify the underlying cause. We always recommend a full vet check if the behaviour is constant, and you have concerns. Keep a diary of the behaviour changes for your vet to review, and for management keep areas and gardens clean where your puppy and dog toilets.

WEEK TWO - GETTING PUPPY SKILLS STARTED

Food Manners by Chirag Patel

You will need 1 small pot filled with treats.

This is where your dog/puppy learns what behaviours pay off around food. You will need to decide what behaviours you want to reinforce around food. Behaviours you may want to see is calm behaviour, sitting, standing, looking at you and distance from food. Behaviours we do not reinforce are jumping up, scratching, biting or barking for example.

- Hold your small bowl high enough away from your dog while kneeling or standing, we want to make this easy for your puppy or dog and feel relaxed around the food at an easy level. When your dog moves away from the bowl, is relaxed or offering any behaviours you want around food, mark the behaviour with a 'marker word' and give your dog a reward from the bowl by offering your dog a treat on an open hand.

- If you find your dog is excited by your hand going into the food bowl, then freeze and wait for a desirable behaviour to reinforce. You can then stretch out your arm with the treat adding further distance for your dog making this exercise a little easier.

- In small steps we want to build this relaxed behaviour around food, so that we can place the bowl on the floor while reinforcing desired behaviours and for our puppy to ignore the bowl. You may need to go back a few steps which is completely normal during learning new skills.

- Don't add cues, for example asking for sit, down etc., we simply want your puppy/dog to learn that you with food or in the presence of food, means that only specific behaviours pay.

Jumping Up – Preventing this unwanted behaviour

Paws on the Floor is a lovely fun expression we use for teaching dogs not to jump up on guests, jumping up at the dining table or becoming excited by visitors that come to the front door. There are many practical reasons for teaching calm door introductions; firstly, elderly guests that may be injured from an exuberant greeting, children being knocked by an overly happy big puppy or parents coming through the door holding their baby. This can be taught by rewarding when paws are on floor and by using a settle spot you dog can be cued to for visitors to enter in a calm way.

We also need to consider dog law and how a dog does not need to bite or injure a person for a complaint to be made to the dog warden or local council. Of course, puppies and dogs make mistakes, as we do, however as owners and pet carers we need to consider management and training to keep other people and our dogs safe and well managed in the human world we share.

Paws On The Floor

- Management is key whilst teaching your dog not to jump up and keep their paws on the floor. A stairgate will help manage the environment whilst you begin training to keep your dog behind calmly and safely. We don't want your dog practising the behaviour of jumping up at visitors.
- If a stairgate is impractical for your home and set up, then you can use a lead on your dog for careful greetings. Reward all calm interaction and paws on the floor.
- Always ignore jumping up which is the simplest way to stop reinforcing the behaviour. Any attention, even negative, pushing the dog away, shouting, will reinforce the unwanted behaviour, which you do not want. Ignoring jumping up is effective, however often during using this method you may find the behaviour increases as your dog tries harder to jump up. Now you are giving him/her no attention and being consistently calm.
- Remain calm, still, arms folded if needed so you are less interesting and exciting. Wait for paws to be on the floor and calm behaviour, gently mark with a yes/good (marker word) and reward with a yummy treat. Continue to reinforce this calmness by dropping treats on the floor for your dog to sniff and eat.
- If your dog begins to jump up once more, continue to ignore, when paws are on the floor, immediately reward, wait a few seconds and once again reward your pup. Being consistent with reinforcement is important.
- Once your dog and you are confident with the paws on the floor training you can move the training forward to teaching this around guests. Once visitors are settled or have come in, your pup can be introduced calmly to family and friends. Continue to reward all calm interactions and behaviour. This will again reinforce paws on the floor behaviour.
- If your dog is a little nervous or unconfident of people visiting, delivery people, or during training keep your dog separate to your guests in a place he/she feels calm and safe with a nice long-lasting treat like a filled Kong or Lickimat. Once visitors are settled then introduce your dog slowly, rewarding all calm behaviour and encouraging your dog to their safe settle space or mat.
- All visitor's safety, from family to delivery people are your responsibility hence management is important at all times during training, as we don't want to set your dog up to fail. Ignoring the unwanted behaviour and rewarding the calm (wanted behaviour) will reinforce a positive greeting.
- With our dogs, we also taught a cue for jumping up, or 'Paws Up'. Placing the behaviour on cue means that the behaviour only occurs when cued. Paws up, we use this as a target for our dog to also move onto surfaces and areas with their paws.

Teaching a 'Drop' Cue

An exchange game or a 'Take/Drop' game is a fun way to not only protect your puppy from a harmful item they may pick up, but also build trust using swapping and exchanges. As mentioned in a previous section on children and dogs, trading is key to prevent guarding behaviours in our dogs.

We like to teach this as a fun game through play with a dog, 'Take and Drop' teaches your dog to **release** an object in his mouth. This is basically an exchange game and is another great way to build trust with your dog. Taking something from your dog can lead to a dog feeling threatened, possibly begin to refuse or guard an object. We want your presence near items, and the addition of a 'Drop' cue to mean to your dog that a yummier or more rewarding item happens or is given and exchanged.

Trading Game with your Dog – Take and Drop

- Firstly, have two toys/objects the same and of low value. Maybe a simple rope toy. Keep one behind your back, or in a back pocket.
- Offer your dog an object or toy of low value. Make the toy move in exciting play. Be careful not to pull the toy to hard, especially with younger puppies as can cause strain.
- As they open their mouth to take the toy, cue; **'Take'**.
- Your dog will begin to play with the toy, ragging or shaking it as you play tug together.
- Stop the game by bringing your arm to the side, stopping movement.
- As your dog continues to play with the toy, they will likely lose a little interest due to the lack of movement and your calmer behaviour. Then pull the hidden double toy out. Your dog will naturally wish to investigate, as soon as they release the first toy, cue; **'Drop'**.
- Immediately reward with the second toy by beginning tug play. And cue; **'Take'**.
- **This is the exchange!**
- As you progress and build on this you may find your dog doesn't wish to trade at some point. In which case, walk away and pick up a new toy. As their curiosity brings them to investigate as you play and they drop the first item/toy, immediately reward with giving them the new toy and cue; **'Take'**. Repeat the game, waiting for release and immediately cue, **'Drop'**.
- Practice trading different items and swapping items for a reward.
- This can also continue on walks when your dog finds unsafe objects you need them to release after building this game at home. Carry high value treats for situations like this of higher distraction. This way when you cue **'Drop'**, your dog automatically knows what you have is really yummy, toys and good stuff!

Note: Using higher value treats and rewards to swap with will encourage this desired behaviour and increase the likelihood your dog will choose the item or reward you have. This is especially useful in situation where your dog through natural exploration picks up something unsafe. A reliable 'drop' could prevent an injury and unwanted behaviour.

Settling and Capturing Calm

One of the first captured behaviours we love to help dog owners with is capturing settling on a mat, bed or area. Being able to visual cue 'rest' and 'relax' is useful in so many settings. Going for a coffee and taking your pet with you, on holiday in a hotel room, a friend's house, recuperating post injury or surgery or settling a puppy that may be over aroused. There are so many useful applications of this lovely simple behaviour.

Having your dog able to relax and settle on cue, on a settlemat, blanket, bed or safe space is a perfect way to lead to a calm dog in different environments and situations. When your dog is overstimulated, anxious, in new place or recouping from injury or illness, this is lovely relaxation training. Imagine having a blanket you can take with you to cafes, restaurants, hotels and appointments that you can place down for your dog to curl up and relax. **Puppies also need to sleep 18-20 hours a day** for healthy development of their central nervous and immune system, the brain and muscles, as well as processing information, aiding learning. **An adult dog will need 12-14 hours per day**, however, if there are changes in your dog's sleeping behaviour, we recommend a vet check to rule out any health concerns.

- Encourage your dog to their settle area. (We find using a specific blanket either on your dog's bed, safe place or a mat means you can more easily transport your settle spot elsewhere.) As your dog gets near, interacts with, places a paw/s, sniffs the settlemat, begin to drop treats on the mat. Stop when the dog moves away from the settlemat.

- Don't mark or click this behaviour as this may excite your dog, as they may then be waiting for another cue or to continue training. We want to promote and encourage calm.

- We are desensitising your dog to the settlemat at this stage so don't worry if your dog moves from the settle place, simply stop rewarding. When your dog's attention is back on the mat, drop the yummy goodies.

- Relax yourself, deep breaths, calm, we find sitting next to the settlemat encourages your dog to do the same. When your dog has all 4 paws, sits, lays down on the mat or blanket, continually reinforce with rapid small treats.

- A great long-lasting reinforcer is Primula squeezy cheese, straight from the tube or squeezed into a Kong which you can hold low as your dog lays and licks. Watch your dog's body language, look for relaxed signs, body language and deeper longer breaths.

- After practising this a number of times with your dog you can take a step back after your dog has relaxed on the mat, leaving them with a longer lasting treat and then add a cue.

- Encourage your dog to his settlemat and cue, 'Settle' or 'Place'. By now you have reinforced that the mat is calm, safe and good place. Leave your dog with a long-lasting yummy treat and move away from them, adding distance. If they follow you, lead them back to their mat and drop treats. When they move off and away from the mat, the yummy things stop.

- If your dog chooses to rest and calm in the settle place, on a blanket/mat you can capture and reinforce by dropping treats onto the mat. Reward choices your puppy or dog offer that are also desired behaviours.

Note: A yummy long-lasting treat is great for continual reinforcement. Licking and chewing will help to promote calmness and another way for your dog to relax.

WEEK THREE – RECALL WEEK

Care needs to be taken on stairs, beds and sofas due to a puppy's soft bones, carry your puppy upstairs to bed to help prevent any potential injuries or strain on joints. Remember to roll balls gently, hold toys for a puppy to pull on but don't tug on the toys to protect their necks. Introduce a puppy soft harness and lead using positive association with rewards and treats. Keep training sessions to 5 minutes which keeps games fun and a puppy enthused, but not overtire them.

Use safety gates and puppy pens to manage the environment and keep your exploring puppy safe.

Reflex to Name/ Recall

A reflex to name is important for a puppy and dog for a look at me or before a cue. It was Ivan Pavlov that studied reflexes and triggers, it is from his work which we base much of our reward-based training. We will be teaching your puppy that their name and coming to you means good things. Having a good solid recall is not only important from a safety aspect but great for your bond and lots of fun too. The key thing is to begin in a low distraction environment as we don't want to set your puppy up to fail. We introduce the 'Counting Game' too.

We want your dog to associate their name with the positive and good things. Teaching your dog to recognise and respond to his/her name is for focus and eye contact with you. Always say their name in a happy positive tone to create a positive association.

- **'Name': Reflex to Name/Word (turn of the head, eye contact) = Reward**

- A reflex to name can be practised at home, whilst walking on lead or at a distance, we are just asking for eye contact. As soon as your dog's eyes or head move upwards or towards you, reward with a treat immediately. This will create an immediate positive feeling to their name and associate good things.

- **Recall Cue:** Think of your cue word for example, 'Come' or 'Here'. Choose which cue word you want to charge up.

- Begin with an environment with no distractions. We don't want to set the dog up to fail or lose our trust. We want to teach your dog that coming to you always means good things. Coming to

TRAINING & BONDING TIPS

My dogs LOVE Liver Cake, it's their Recall Reward! Here is a great recipe:

1 lb (450g) raw liver (lambs or pigs)
1 lb (450g) granary flour (or gluten-free flour for dogs with allergies)
3 eggs
One teaspoon of vegetable oil and a
Dash of milk

Liquidise liver with eggs, milk and oil in blender until smooth. Add to flour and mix well. Pop into a greased baking tray. Bake at 180 deg for 35-45 Minutes. Allow to cool then cut into pieces.

you always needs to be rewarded with high value food or a high value toy that has been charged with play every time the dog sees it.

- Slowly increase distance, from room to room, practice in the garden, then build up to outside on walks with the long line. Practice for short bursts, so neither of you get bored or frustrated with the exercise.

- **Cue your dog's name 'Name'** at a short distance, which has now been charged with good things, wait for a reflex to their name, looking at you or eye contact. Immediately mark with your marker, then cue your recall word, **'Come'** and move backwards. As your dog moves towards you, stop, mark again and drop treats in front of your feet.

- Once the behaviour becomes reliable you can build further distance and practice in different environments, adding distraction.

- **Remember to practice touching the harness/collar gently when your dog recalls to you** and you have dropped treats that your dog is sniffing and eating. This will desensitise your dog to the feeling of restraint for when you do need to clip the lead back on. Then practice dropping treats, clipping lead back on, drop a few more treats and unclip and release your dog. When the time comes to leave a field or activity you will have a dog that is comfortable with this process.

The Back-and-Forth Game

- Start in a low distraction environment, the home or garden. One person gains your dog's attention, plus a nice opportunity to practice and reward eye contact. In a happy, excited tone the Second person at a distance cue's the dog's 'Name' then the recall word for e.g., 'Come'. As soon as he/she begins to recall to you, mark the behaviour and reward with treats or play a fun game of tug. This is also a great game to engage your dog on walks.

- Once you have charged the recall verbal cue you can then build on this with a hand signal you can add in at the same time. This is useful in noisy environments and for greater distances. Again, like previous exercises slowly build upon recall, as the key is to charge the recall cue.

- Do not worry, or get angry, if your dog does not respond. Try not to chase your dog unless an emergency and use the 'crazy human run' to entice your dog back playfully, dog's love to chase and movement will motivate them to come back to you.

- On a recall return, drop treats as well and touch your puppy or dog's collar or harness. This will help desensitise this process of needing to clip the lead back on, helping make your dog feel more comfortable touching their collar or harness. You can also clip the lead back on, reward again and then unclip the lead and release your dog. This will teach your dog that the fun and good things don't stop when the lead is put back on. Once on lead sprinkle some treats to find in long grass.

- Have fun on your walks, be a focus of play. The environment does not have to be the only source of stimulation. You can be too! Take a special or novel tug toy or flirt pole with you on walks. Your dog when unclipped off lead will want to play with you, rather than just run into the environment or search for other dogs.

- Distractions occur, and no dog has 100% recall. But slowly building the recall from a distraction free environment will give your dog a greater chance for success. Build your levels slowly. Go back a stage or decrease distance and distraction if your dog does not respond.

- Please email us at any time you wish to further training skills or need to change or adapt the technique or plan. Always begin with minimal distraction, let your dog guide you and do not worry about going back a step as this is perfectly normal, we still adjust working with our own dogs.

Chirag Patel's Counting Game

This game is one that we love teaching and puppies and dogs like playing. It's one to teach in low distraction in your home, move to the garden or a near outside space on a longline of not enclosed and then build into new environments, along with your recall.

The game is simple, as you count in a clear voice, drop treats in front of your feet. This will give your dog a jackpot on returning to you but also a fun game without overusing their name. It also gives you an idea of how distracting an environment is. Higher the count = More distractions.

Now we don't expect you to drop 68 treats as you reach the count of 68, but do keep on counting and doing the action of dropping treats. We usually stop dropping treats between 5-10, so there is still a big jackpot and pay out for your dog.

- Prep lots of small treats in your treat bag or pouch.

- Wait for your puppy/dog to be distracted elsewhere in the room.

- Start by saying a count of '1' out loud and drop a treat near your feet, then '2' and drop a treat, '3' and drop a treat, '4' and drop a treat. '5' and drop a treat, and so on, creating a small jackpot pile or rewards.

- When your dog approaches you, starts sniffing, immediately stop counting and placing treats into the counted pile.

- Move away, wait for you dog to finish his jackpot and start the game again.

- Note the reduction in counts as your puppy or dog learns this fun game. It's lots of fun as part of your recall toolbox and is a lovely way to teach your puppy or dog coming to you and being near you mean good things.

- You can play this game in groups and with the family spaced out. Your puppy or dog will then need to listen who and where the counting is coming from. Children love getting involved with this game.

Rolling Recall Game – a foundation to teaching a 'middle'.

A fun and simple game, that builds in automatic check ins and engagement and a foundation to 'Middle'. Prep some treats in your treat bag for this game.

- Throw a treat in a rolling movement close to your dog. Once your dog turns, sniffs and begins to eat the treat, as soon as they begin to turn around to engage back with you, cue your check in/recall cue such as 'Come' or 'Here'.
- As soon as your dog reaches you roll/throw a treat in the opposite direction, where your dog will run past you.
- Once again, when your dog turns back to you, cue your check in/recall cue and roll the treat in the opposite direction.
- Repeat this a few times, then begin a cool down. Where you cue your check in/recall cue but instead of rolling a treat, sprinkle some in the grass or floor.

Next, we can add a bridge/middle using our legs as a tunnel.

- Throw a rolling treat towards your dog to engage them into the game.
- Wait for your dog to sniff, find and eat the yummy treat, as soon as they turn back towards you and the good things (treats), cue your check in/recall cue.
- As your dog gets closer to you, throw the treat through your legs, in the opposite direction. Your dog should run through your legs, but don't worry if they run around the outside. If this happens, slow the game down, use a larger treat for your dog to see rolled through your legs.
- Wait again, cue your recall/check in cue, and roll a treat back through your legs in the opposite direction.
- Once your dog becomes confident running through your legs following the rolling treat, you can add a second cue for this behaviour after your recall/check in cue. I use 'through', which means pass through my legs.
- Don't forget a cool-down, ending the session, perhaps with a treat sprinkle for your puppy or dog to sniff. End on a success and keep training sessions to 3-5 minutes.

Hand Target/Touch Cue

The touch cue or hand target is a fun way to focus your dog, it can be used for recall, moving your dog off furniture or objects, various tricks like turning on light switches and closing doors. It's also a great start for husbandry as a touch can be used as a way to communicate between dog owner and dog. Whilst your puppy is happy focusing on you with a hand touch you can slowly carry out husbandry, for e.g., grooming, paw inspection, nail clipping. When the puppy breaks from a hand touch, the husbandry stops for your dog to take a pause. This will help build trust and help communication.

The **'Touch'** cue can also be used if you want your dog to touch items, objects or things with his nose. It's a fun and simple cue to teach which has so many uses, for example indicating in Scentwork, target touching, assistance dog work, trick training, as part of recall and much more. It's also a lovely way to focus your dog onto you in possible fearful situations, from other dogs and high distraction environments. This will give your dog a positive cue to focus on until the fear of perhaps people, other dogs or a situation passes. As well as for fun to exercise your dog's clever mind.

- Present and show your flat hand to your dog in front of them. We like to hide a treat in-between our fingers to add interest. As they go to curiously investigate your hand and touch it with their nose, mark the nose touch with a 'Yes' or 'Good' (your charged marker word) and reward them with a treat from the other hand and treat bag.

- Remove your hand and place by your side, offer your hand once more and wait. Again, as your dog touches your hand with their nose, mark and reward.

- Repeat this exercise until your dog is touching your hand whenever you present it.

- When your dog begins to offer the behaviour consistently, as he goes to touch your hand with his nose start adding the cue; 'Touch'. After many repetitions you will find that he will associate the cue with the action of touching your hand.

- When he is reliably touching your hand, use this cue around the home. Call your dog to come to you, and as he gets close, extend your hand and cue them to, 'Touch.'

- Every touch needs to be rewarded. Reward your dog! This is where a treat pouch comes in handy!

- When your dog is responding well indoors, take the exercise outside where there are more distractions, like your garden. Build this slowly and don't be afraid to go back a step.

- Gradually increase the distance between you and your dog so that your dog has to travel further to touch your hand. This can be used as part of recall training.

WEEK FOUR – CUES TO KEEP YOUR PUPPY SAFE

Teaching a 'Stay'

As a dog owner with large dog breeds, it was important to teach a pause through doorways and gates so that myself, family, and guests can pass through safely with being knocked over or injured.

A Stay cue has many useful applications, from teaching door manners, opening gates on walks and safe introductions to safety in situations where you may be near a road, different distractions or come across something on a walk you need to assess before releasing your dog from a lead or release cue.

Teaching a Stay Cue

A **'Stay'** cue is useful as a pause before a release or another cue. **The release cue is as important as the stay cue and will reinforce the stay cue.** For us having our large breed of dog pause before a gate or door whilst we open the gate is much safer, it means we are not pushed to one side trying to carry shopping or pulled over. Plus, it can give us a pause to look for example for livestock in a field before entering, or other dogs and stimuli in a field you may not see without first checking if off lead.

We like to start this near a doorway or back door to the garden. Or practice on a mat so there is specific visual position for you to begin.

Step 1: Encourage your puppy or dog to sit near the doorway or mat and reward, keep rewarding this position with a high rate of reinforcement. **Staying in position = Good things, food/treats.**

Practice this step, building duration in the chosen position over a number of sessions before increasing distance.

Step 2: Building distance: Take a small step back through the doorway/mat or away from the chosen position, then immediately return to your puppy or dog and reward again with a jackpot of treats.

Set your criteria, your dog may move slightly, a shift in posture for comfort, but the criteria needs to be where your dog does not move from the position you want them to 'stay'/pause.

This may be half a step away from your dog. We need to build distance slowly so that our stay position becomes reliable and to reinforce the behaviour we want. If your puppy or dog moves from the position or towards you, simply encourage your puppy back to the first position and start from the beginning. You may need to go back a step which is normal when practising new behaviours.

Build this distance into 2 steps, then 3 steps moving back from your and reward on return.

Step 3: Adding distraction: Begin moving away from your dog from a different angle, slowly building previous steps. If your dog moves, turns around, rest your dog and go back a few steps. Once you can move away from your dog at different angles, trying walking around your dog while they stay in position. Keep adding distractions slowly.

Step 4: Once you have your puppy or dog waiting until you return reliably without moving, staying in the reinforced and rewarded position, you can add the cue, **'Stay'** or a word/whistle/hand signal you wish to use, before moving away from your dog.

Reliable Stay for Door/Gate Safety

Adding a Release Cue

Once your dog is reliably staying on cue with duration and distance (Step 1 and 2), we like add a release cue. We use **'Through'** or **'Free'** as a release cue.

Step 1: Cue your dog to **'Stay'** with a verbal cue, or a chosen hand signal. Move away a short distance from your dog.

Step 2: Using your hand holding a treat as a visual cue for your dog to follow, throw a treat forward with your hand in forward motion, away from the door or stay position your dog is in and cue a release word, **'Through/Free'**. This acts as a release cue to the Stay cue, which will reinforce the pause. You can phase out the lure and hand movement as your dog learns the release cue, as your dog releases reliably with the 'Through/Free' cue and moves from the stay position.

Tip: You can build behaviour this to an outside back door, cue 'Stay' and follow this with the release cue, 'Through/Free', where you dog moves through the door and into the garden. Then incorporate into walks and moving through gates and other areas. Practice all new behaviours in new environments safely using a comfortable well fit harness and long line lead.

Exchanges and Swapping – safety around items

We continue exchanges and start by offering an exchange of a lower value item for a higher one. For example, an older toy/a yoghurt pot/slipper for a yummy piece of chicken or sausage. We want your puppy to know that humans mean good things. Which is why we never take a dog's food. And we should ask, why would you want to? We want to build trust and for our dogs to learn and know that humans being around food mean positive things happen. Not, that our presence means we take things, especially their meals away from them.

Teaching a Leave – a backchain method (see notes at end of book)

This important cue is needed in so many situations. Like recall a good, reliable 'Leave It' is important for many safety reasons like a drop. A Leave means for your dog to take their nose away from something, disengage and engage with you. Something unknown could be a hazard to your puppy or dog and by teaching this cue and building distraction slowly incredible useful for all dog owners.

Teaching a **'Leave'** is an important cue for puppies and dogs to protect your dog from harm and useful for times your dog may be investigating something tasty on your kitchen floor that may not be safe. A great cue to prevent your dog from picking up, licking, or sniffing things that maybe dangerous on a walk or to stop a dog bin raid. It can have other applications for example, ignoring stimulus after being cued to 'Leave' if your dog becomes excitable to then focus on you. It's also important to capture and reward calm behaviour and behaviour we want to see.

Start with the Behaviour we do want

- Encourage your dog to sit in front of you and reward calm relaxed behaviour.
- Once your dog is focused on you, or offers eye contact, mark or click with a clicker and reward.
- Continue to mark, click for focus/eye contact in a short repetition of 10-20.

Adding Distraction

- After following the above, as your dog is focused on you, move one of your hands to the side with your hand closed (a low distraction), wait for focus on you/eye contact, mark or click and reward. Repeat this. We are looking for your dog to ignore your movement and distraction.
- Once this is reliable, build to moving your arm to the side, lowering to the floor and open your hand, mimicking dropping something. Again, as soon as your dog is focused on you, offering eye contact. Mark or click and reward.

- Once this is reliable and your dog is ignoring your movement and hand, you can add a further distraction. In the hand you open drop a low value toy. Mark or click focus on you/eye contact or a check in.

Adding the Cue

- Once you have built this slowly you can add the cue.
- Move your arm with the toy to the side and drop.
- Cue **'Leave'**.
- Mark and Reward focus on you and eye contact or check in.

Remember to always reward the behaviour we want to reinforce. You can add further items to for your dog to leave, once reliability has been built. Different toys and then build to food.

Engagement and focus – capturing voluntary eye contact

Loose Lead Foundations Part 1

Loose lead walking is one of the top behaviours that trainers are asked for support in. It can be difficult for dogs to learn and understand what we want from them on lead. Trainers and behaviourists do not recommend tools that stop pulling, such as headcollars, figure of 8 and slip leads for example as they work by adding something unpleasant to suppress behaviour.

Loose lead is a skill we needed to teach, so we are not pulled about on lead by strong dogs which could cause the handler injury. Pulling can also cause tension and strain for the dog as well. Loose lead does take a long time and lots of reinforcement, but worth the training for lovely walks.

So, what is loose lead? For us, this simply means no tension on the lead. But for our dogs we're asking a lot from them. Checking in with us, eye contact, awareness of their body around us, walking and also simply being a dog and being able to sniff on walks.

Luring or Lure-reward training is a highly effective way to teach your dog new behaviours. It is easy and fun for both dog and human, and dogs can learn new behaviours quite quickly with this training. This type of training simply involves using a food reward to guide the dog into the desired position or behaviour. If your dog is not motivated by food, you can use toys instead.

Luring works because food makes dogs feel good, and a strong motivator will help a dog focus, learn, and enjoy the training with you. With patience, good timing, and frequent repetition, you can teach your dog all kinds of new behaviours using food rewards. Here we use a lure to encourage our dog into a position near us.

- Begin training loose lead with no harness or lead, because all you want to capture is a positive association to being near you and engagement. Starting in a known low distraction environment in the home, then moving to the garden.

- Whilst building this behaviour you will get through many treats but keep sessions short to 5 minutes or less. As you will be in a low distraction environment, which is an area known with little distractions by your dog, you can use lower value rewards. I often use a dried treat as my dogs can become very focused and aroused by the food. When you take new skills to another new environment you may need to up the reward value.

- Firstly, simply drop treats near you so the dog associates being near and around you with good things.

- When your puppy/dog looks at you, offers eye contact and checks in, mark and reward. By rewarding this wanted behaviour, your dog will likely repeat it, as it pays with a treat.

- Begin by luring your dog into a position near you, release the treat from your hand and reward. Mark and reward any offered engagement behaviour or eye contact, even if brief.

- We use a verbal marker word while working on loose lead to keep hands free to just deliver treats. Sometimes hands can become confused trying to click with a clicker and reward, hence a verbal marker word is useful.

   (Note: Secondary Reinforcer: Marker Word/Clicker is paired with a **Primary Reinforcer: Food.** The clicker or marker word needs charging before using.

   Good = Treat (repeat 10-15 times daily as a little exercise, click then treat))

   Mark eye contact, along with rewarding your dog's choice and position to be near you.

   Being Near You = Good Things.

- Once you have rewarded and captured these behaviours a few times, throw a treat away from you. This gives your dog the choice to return to you and continue training together and repeat the building behaviours. **Giving our dogs choices builds confidence** and helps develop these skills.

- Then you can build to taking a step forward and having your dog follow you, continuing to mark and reward eye contact and check ins. Then every 2 steps, 3, 4. 5 and so on.

   Keep sessions short and end on a success. Once this has been slowly built you can then add in more movement and the 'follow me' loose lead skills.

WEEK FIVE – HUSBANDRY AND COOPERATIVE CARE FOCUS

This week we look at cooperative husbandry and care which rests on your trust and bond with your puppy that you will be building every day. In Lisa Tenzin-Dolma's book, 'Heartbeat at your Feet', 2012; p56, Lisa states, "Training is a two-way street. We need the cooperation of our dogs for training to be effective and long-lasting, and the best way to ensure cooperation is to gain the dog's trust and affection to make training fun."

Husbandry and General Pet Care

Husbandry and handling of your puppy and dog is essential for not only day to day care but vet visits, health care, administering medicine and treatment if needed. Cooperative offered behaviours trained using positive reinforcement can lower stress of these types of handling. We do this by building trust and communication, a target touch and yummy rewards. Primula tubes of squeezy cheese are useful for longer reinforcement plus a calming treat. The 'Chase 'n Chomp Sticky Bone' is a great treat toy for bathing, grooming and clipping nails.

The Bucket Game.

Chirag Patel, an animal behaviourist created and introduced 'The Bucket Game' to encourage a conversation between animals and people. It can be used not only for husbandry training and caregiving behaviours, but also as a confidence builder, relaxation and for fun. It builds trust and communication and something that is useful to take out in everyday life and situations.

What's on your dog training bucket list?
The fun and easy dog training game made to empower the learners and offer choice.

We create an environment where our dogs have choice and can tell us:
- when they are ready to start
- when they want to take a break
- when they want to stop
- when they want us to slow down

This game was initially designed to teach essential husbandry behaviours, (those behaviours that allow your dog to actively participate in their daily and veterinary care). But you will soon learn how this game can be integrated into your everyday training to help reduce barking, increase confidence and enhance your overall relationship.

Designed by Internationally respected animal training & behaviour consult, Chirag Patel; 'The Bucket Game' makes dog training fun, easy and truly allows you to have a 'conversation' with your dog. The game is based on behavioural principles used in animal training.

Foundation of the Game:
Your dog will focus on the bucket, keeping their face 1-2 feet away and out of the bucket. They will focus towards the bucket to signal they are ready to start a training conversation with you and will

remove their focus to signal you to stop, take a break or change the speed of the conversation. Your dog gets to start making some choices such as the ones mentioned above as well as whether they stand, sit, or lies down.

This game uses shaping, targeting, stationing and many other behavioural principles in a way that makes it fun for both the animal and the care giver.

YouTube Video: https://www.youtube.com/watch?v=GJSs9eqi2r8

What you will need:

- A bucket (size appropriate for your puppy or small pot)
- Rewards (high value treats chopped small)
- A bed/settlemat or safe place
- Once settled into a relaxed position place the bucket filled with treats down.
- When your dog looks at the bucket, give them a treat from the bucket. Repeat this whenever your dog is focused on the bucket.
- If your dog chooses to move away from the settlemat/area stop the reinforcement and wait for your dog to be ready and engaged again.
- Once your dog is comfortable with the game you can decide what husbandry behaviour you want to concentrate on, for example an ear check.
- When your dog moves its focus away from the bucket move your hand way, wait for your dog to be focused again on the bucket, reward and continue moving your hand closer to your dog's ear.
- Build the game slowly, this about a conversation and building trust slowly.

Stand Cue – How we can use hand target too.

Teaching a 'Stand' cue has many uses, from veterinary inspections, as well as grooming and husbandry care. We can do this in a few ways, using a lure, marking, rewarding and then adding a cue. Or capturing the behaviour, marking, reinforcing the behaviour and then adding a cue. We can also use our hand target cue to move a dog into a stand position comfortably.

Using a Lure

Step 1: Begin by asking or luring your dog into sit or down position, if your dog is comfortable with these positions. Many dogs are not comfortable in which case capturing a stand may be more suitable for your dog.

Step 2: Have a yummy treat in your hand and let your dog sniff it. As your dog is sniffing the treat, use the treat to lure your dog in a horizontal movement away from them, keeping the treat near their nose until they stand. Immediately mark the stand with a click/marker word and reward your dog with the treat.

Step 3: Repeat step 2 for a few repetitions over 3–5-minute training sessions, until your dog is reliably and comfortably moving into a stand position when lured with the treat.

Step 4: Adding a Voice Cue. Once your dog is standing reliably when lured with the treat, it's time to introduce voice cue. Using a treat to lure from the sit/down position, move your palm away from your dog's nose and add the verbal cue "Stand". Then reward with treats from your other hand, rather than using the treat lure.

Step 5: Adding a Hand Signal. This is useful to add for deaf puppies and dogs. Lure as before in movement, moving your open flat palm away from your dog's nose. (Your dog will likely be reliably following the hand from luring in previous steps and releasing the treat). Now progress to using this movement as the hand signal with your palm moving away from your dog's nose without a treat in your hand, mark with a click/marker word and reward once your dog is in the stand position from the other hand.

You may find your dog ignores the hand movement and remains in a sit/down. If this happens, tuck a treat between your palm and your thumb and repeat the hand signal, moving your palm in a slower movement which will act as lure. Then reward from your other hand. Repeat a few times until your dog is reliably offering the behaviour. Then use the same hand movement, but with no tucked treat and reward from your other hand, this will fade out the lure.

Step 6: You can practice both methods separately or at the same time if you wish to teach your dog with a verbal and hand signal. You can cue a verbal "Stand" and use the hand signal at the same time, particularly if your dog is struggling with one of the cues. Then phase out either one once the behaviour and cue are paired. Remember to mark the behaviour and reward each time. You can then begin to build duration by marking and then delivering the treat a few seconds after. This can be built slowly and is useful for vet and grooming visits.

Capturing a Stand

Step 1: Wait for your puppy or dog to offer a stand, paws on the floor and still.

Begin to rapidly offer them treats near their mouth. Mark the behaviour with a click or marker word, capturing the wanted behaviour. If the dog moves any foot out of position, stop the rewards. As soon as they stand still again with all four paws on the floor, begin to offer treats and mark the behaviour.

Practise this in short sessions of 3-5 minutes, heavily rewarding your dog and marking the behaviour for standing still.

Step 2: Once you have practised this over a few sessions you can then see if your dog will offer a stand. During a session, stop rewarding the stand position. Your dog will likely offer different behaviours, possibly a sit for example. You can reward the sit with one treat. But don't mark this behaviour.

Next: Wait for your dog to offer the stand position which has been heavily rewarded with a big payment in your previous steps. As soon as your dog stands, mark and reinforce again with lots of yummy treats rapidly given. We are looking for your dog at this stage to make the link that offering a stand position will mean lots of treats, a big payment! This will reinforce the action of standing up, *after* your dog has had lots of reinforcement for duration standing.

Step 3: Adding a Cue. Once your dog is moving reliably from one position to a stand position you can add a cue. If your dog is in a sit, reward with one treat, cue a "Stand", wait for your dog to move into the stand position which has been reinforced during previous sessions, mark and reward again with lots of treats. Don't repeat the cue, wait for the behaviour.

Muzzle Training

Dogs that are used to wearing muzzles are trained using reward-based methods to feel comfortable wearing them. The safest type of dog muzzle is a basket-based muzzle – its open basket design allows the dog to breathe freely and take treats, pant, and drink. Other types of muzzles that completely close a dog's mouth, do not allow them to pant or to lose heat, these are not recommended or safe to use.

Make sure you get the correct size for your dog. The piece that goes across the nose must not rub their eyes and many brands are padded so will not rub the dog's nose.

As well enabling you to feel more relaxed and keeping everyone safe and for vet visits, muzzle training has the potential added benefit of helping your dog avoid situations that may worry them, as people are less likely to approach you both. Certain health conditions require a dog to wear a muzzle, for example, if your dog cannot risk picking up food items up on walks and eating them.

It is very important that although your dog has a muzzle on, you should still try to avoid situations they are uncomfortable in, as being exposed to scary or fearful situations could make their behaviour worse in the long term, as well as cause stress. Dogs can learn to feel comfortable wearing muzzles just in the same way that they learn to accept wearing their collar by desensitising them slowly, and by taking your time to introduce them in a positive and fun way.

Helping your Dog feel comfortable putting their nose/muzzle into an enclosed space:

What you will need:

- **Large Yoghurt Pots**
- **Squeezy Primula cheese**
- **Comfortable muzzle**
- **Treats**

Place a little squeezy cheese into a yoghurt pot near the lip entrance and let your dog investigate and sniff the pot, licking the cheese. Continue to do this for short sessions, building duration and placing the cheese further into the pot. This step helps dogs that maybe have not been comfortable previously with muzzles. We then build to placing the yoghurt pot into the basket muzzle and doing the same exercise.

If your dog has not begun any muzzle training you can begin at this step, or do both. Use the muzzle as though it is a small bowl for your dog to eat their treats out of. Cup the muzzle in your hand and drop a treat into it, so that your hand prevents it from falling out. Allow your dog to put their face into the muzzle to take the treat. Repeat this several times – your dog will be learning to really love putting their face inside the muzzle and create a positive association with the muzzle.

Muzzle = Food Reward/Good things

We then want to build duration slowly with the muzzle. Hold the muzzle up for your dog to see and wait for your dog to choose to place their face into the muzzle. Once they do, wait a few seconds and reward. Extend this slowly during short muzzle training session, delaying the treat, waiting and rewarding. If your dog chooses to move away from the muzzle, go back a few steps and reward for a shorter duration.

Targeting face into Muzzle = Food Reward/Good Things

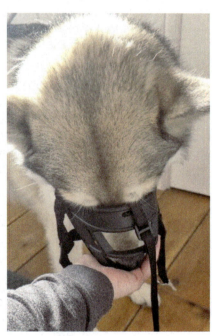

Desensitising to wearing the Muzzle Fully and Straps:

Once your dog is choosing every time to place their face into a muzzle when presented we then want to begin to desensitise them to have the straps place over their face and head. This needs to be slowly and carefully. Placing 1 strap at a time over gently then removing whilst rewarding your dog. Once your dog is fully comfortable, relaxed and still choosing to keep their face in the muzzle you can then build to clicking or buckling the straps. This needs to be done at your dog's individual pace. Looking for any stress signs. Any attempt your dog makes to remove their face from the muzzle, go back a few steps and slowly build steps again.

Muzzle = Good Things/Positive Association.

Loose Lead Skills Part 2 – Beginning 'Follow Me' on Lead

We will teach a lovely fun and simple technique for you to teach your puppy loose lead, having no tension and enjoying walking near you. We want you as the dog owner to be the source of good things, we keep marking and rewarding eye contact and check ins that your puppy or dog gives you.

Is your dog comfortable with equipment? Have you desensitised your dog slowly to wearing a harness and the feel of a trailing lead? For this technique use a longer lead or a longline. Do not be afraid to go back a few steps with any parts of training. Uncomfortable and poorly fit equipment can cause discomfort and may exacerbate unwanted behaviour, such as pulling.

Wolf and Whippet are fully reward-based trainers and therefore we do not recommend using any tools, such as slip leads, figure of 8, headcollars etc. to suppress pulling behaviour on lead. These tools work by adding something unpleasant to suppress behaviour, discomfort, tension and often pain to the nose, muzzle and neck of a dog. Instead, we recommend fun training that captures focus and engagement.

- Practice using a nice loose long lead/line in the garden. Always use a harness to protect the soft tissue of your dog's neck and trachea from potential injury. A long line is great whilst practising this method as you dog will automatically be on a loose lead with no tension due to the longer lead. We will also need to look at why a puppy or dog is pulling and how pulling is being reinforced. Often the environment is very exciting, and dogs will pull towards scent and stimuli.

- Have your puppy or dog follow you as you walk backwards on a nice long loose lead, while reinforcing them with treats in front of you. This will teach and reinforce them that being near you and following you, both mean good things. If your dog is following you, they won't be pulling you. Once your dog is responding well and following happily build to moving to a side position, adjusting your bodies position slowly while reinforcing the behaviour with yummy treat rewards to your side. This is where your previous foundations are key, capturing eye contact and check-ins.

- **Top Tip:** For smaller dogs you can use a target stick or ball flinger with squeezy cheese squeezed on it to deliver a yummy reward.

- Work on this exercise daily for 5 minutes at a time and slowly build to a side position. At any point your dog loses focus or is ahead of you with lead tension, stop, wait for your dog to engage back with you and immediately mark, move backwards and reward your dog. Continue to mark and reward eye contact and being near you. Don't be afraid to go back a step with the follow me technique.

- Once you are both confident in the garden with the technique on a long line, move to the front garden or space using a training lead (a lead you can adjust lengths), along the road and back, around the block, then introduce this into your on-lead walks, slowly building your length of walk. Think of your walk as a bubble which you slowly extend and build loose lead walking into. From to the end of the road, to around the corner, a small loop, until you can walk loose lead around the block. Changing the environment, changes the level of distraction so remember you may need to increase your rate of reinforcement. From rewarding every step and check in, to every other step, every 3 steps, every 4 and so on. However, you may need to change this rate of reinforcement with distraction, rewarding every loose lead step.

- Making walks more interactive and stimulating: We use scentwork and play in every walk rather than always free running and playing. Take some cheese or some smelly treats with you and when you come across a tree press some cheese into the nooks at different levels, with your hand guide your dog towards the scent with a 'Find It'. This is a great way to break up walks and to focus, especially post a high energy play, run or overstimulation.

- Trek off the path, encourage your dog to sniff in bushes and undergrowth, sprinkle treats into long grasses or as we say 'Natures Snufflemat'. Fun, dog lead walks are great, especially for puppies, young dogs with energy and working breeds, as low impact and encouraging your dog to use their nose. Your dog will then be ready to focus on your short training sessions practising loose lead.

This is a really fun and relaxed method which dogs enjoy, as well as building engagement with our dog which will also benefit many other behaviours such as recall. Remember while you begin loose lead walking training to reinforce and reward the desired behaviour with a high rate of reinforcement when we begin teaching loose lead. Giving your dogs feedback, marking behaviour and rewarding more regularly has been shown to achieve better results, along with focus on the handler. Once your dog is offering check-ins regularly with distraction you can change the rate of reinforcement to rewarding every 2 steps with loose lead, then every 3 for example.

Premack Principle, 1959

"More probable behaviours will reinforce less probable behaviours". Your dog will find the environment and natural scents a more reinforcing behaviour/activity (higher value and probability) than loose lead walking and calm behaviour on lead (lower probability behaviour) which we can use. When your dog has a nice loose lead let them sniff in the bushes/on posts/trees. If your dog suddenly pulls or lunges, stop, use your lead skills, wait for them to turn back to you, check-in, mark with a "Good" and continue walking. Loose Lead = Sniffing in the environment. Remain stationary when your dog is sniffing, this way they do not learn that pulling gets them where they want to go next or sniff.

WEEK SIX – LET'S PRACTICE OUR SKILLS

Recap on Cues and Behaviours from previous weeks

Our final week and time to recap and move our behaviours and training forward by changing one of the **'3 D's', distance, duration or distraction**. Build your new behaviours slowly and do not be afraid to go back a few steps.

Practicing Recall Skills by adding distraction

We will practice our charged cue and counting game around other puppies and dogs in class, or on a training walk safely on longlines on a harness or in an outside space. If you are following this guide, practice recall safely, always ask other owners if their dog is happy to be greeted by your puppy, dog, keeping your puppy safe from a potential negative experience.

Loose Lead Walking – using your foundations and follow me technique

Practising around other dogs and real-life distractions to build our lead skills. For owners following this guide at home practice your loose lead on a known part of a usual dog walk. Spend 5 – 10 minutes on each walk working on your loose lead skills. Remember to mark and reward all your dog's check-ins and eye contact.

And lastly a fun and mindful activity to try on walks…

The Backpack Walk

Steve Mann from the IMDT came up with this idea after observing roaming dogs in Peru, noting that they don't run and instead seek out humans during the day to be nearby. The Backpack Walk focuses on letting dogs just 'be', and how they like to just 'be' with us.

The Backpack Walk is conditional on a safe space that your dog feels relaxed in, a short amount of time, so great for times when you are limited due to the weather or busy, plus avoiding things that your dog is scared of. It is great for people that perhaps feel guilty they can't walk their dog for long, sensitive dogs that perhaps are struggling and dog's that are easily overstimulated.

You will need:

1. A quiet corner of a field, a secure field, your garden, somewhere your dog feels safe and relaxed.

2. A Backpack.

3. Small tubs; one containing a novel scent (like the fabric I infuse with cloves for scentwork) and one with a novel food, (grated cheese or carrot for e.g.).

4. A chew; perhaps a dried rabbit ear from Natural Treats Bristol for e.g. My dogs love these and they don't take too long.

5. Take a Lickimat with you with some peanut butter, when you find a bench or place to stop, set the Lickimat up for your dog. The licking will help her relax and also create positive associations in the environment.

6. A novel toy, like a tuggy from Tug-E-Nuff. My dogs love the sheepskin tug toys which I keep just for walks.

Next:

1. Have your dog on a long line, or long loose lead, backpack on your back, with your treat bag on your waist. The environment needs to be pressure and worry free for you both.

2. Relax and let your dog wander and sniff the grass, reward check ins with food rewards, throw the treat into the grass next to you.

3. While your dog is sniffing and eating the treat, move, slowly jogging backwards, encouraging your dog to follow, or gently recall your dog and drop treats at your feet. Continue doing this a few times within a triangle so you stay in the small area.

4. Then sit down, on a bench, tree, or rock. Keep your dog on the long line. Take your time, slowly take the backpack and open it, taking out the tub containing the new scent. Make sure you express excitement, showing your dog how exciting this scent is, giving it lots of attention, sparking your dog's curiosity. Smell the scent yourself and then offer it to them so they can sniff. Then slowly close and return to the backpack. Putting the items back into the backpack is key to this activity.

5. Take out one of the items, the Lickimat of tug toy for example, slowly from the backpack. Again, express your excitement, that this object is really special, let your dog sniff, lick and hold it. After they have finished investigating the item, place it back carefully into the backpack.

6. Then the food! Open the small tub slowly, letting your dog sniff it, perhaps sniff yourself too. Feed your dog little bits, perhaps have a nibble yourself, sprinkle into the grass. Then return the tub back to the backpack.

7. Time for the chew. Get your dog's interest once more and give your dog the yummy chew. Sit close to your dog, if they are relaxed with the food, gently stroke your dog.

8. Pack everything away in the backpack, stand up and wander slowly in the small safe space, retracing your steps and letting your dog sniff.
This exercise is all about mindfulness for you and your canine companion. Focusing on the present, calmly being aware of one's feeling, thoughts and body. A time to take a breath, relax and simply 'be' with each other. Note what happens before and after your walk, has your dog been stressed on the walk there? Were there dogs in the environment leading to trigger stacking, a noisy road? If so, driving to the safe space may be better as this activity needs to be calm and mindful.

Avoid ball flingers and taking a ball on every walk with your puppy or dog. Balls and ball chasing can lead to adrenaline highs, over arousal and excitement, which can escalate to compulsive behaviours, overstimulation and repetitive physical injury to our dogs from chasing balls. Change your walks, hide treats in high grass, lay a treat trail and encourage your dog to find the food, work on some training in different environments and have fun with your recall games.

Cues and Behaviours

All things can be cues when we look at behaviour, visual, verbal or environmental for example. A cue tells our dogs that it is time to execute a behaviour for the chance of reinforcement. (Karen Pryor) The definition of the word 'cue' is:

1. on cue

2. a signal or reminder to do something.
3. *psychology*

the part of any sensory pattern that is identified as the signal for a response.

4. the part, function, or action assigned to or expected of a person.

According to Burch and Bailey (How Dog's Learn, 1999), Skinner wrote "…to adequately demonstrate what was happening between an individual and the environment, three things must be specified" the *antecedent stimuli*, the *behaviour* and the *reinforcing consequence*. These three elements are referred to as *"contingencies of reinforcement"*.

The A, B, C's

A – Antecedent – happening or existing before something else. Cue, signal, sign, word or condition that influence the occurrence of the behaviour.

B – Behaviour – (Or the criteria) can be described as the way in which a person, organism, or group responds to a certain set of conditions.

C – Consequence – the relationship between a result and its cause, cause and effect. The outcome that occurs immediately following the behaviour.

L – Latency – the time between the antecedent and the performance of the behaviour.

So, let's think about this in terms of teaching our dogs new cues and behaviours. We need to consider exactly what a cue will mean for our canine companions. What behaviour are you teaching?

For example, what does a 'Wait' mean? For our dog's it means a pause, do not move forward. The key to training is not to move too quickly, work on capturing, shaping, luring a behaviour until it becomes reliable and then adding a cue. We also have to think about reinforcement, type of reward and environment. Teaching the cue in different environments may require going back a few steps, or 'proofing' the behaviour.

Use this table to keep a note of what each cue you use means for your puppy or dog, what behaviour is the consequence of the cue.

CUE	BEHAVIOUR
(Antecedent: cue before the behaviour)	(Behaviour observed or wanted)
e.g. Down (verbal) Hand is moved lower (visual)	Dog lays down. (Think about shaping/luring behaviour.)

CUE	BEHAVIOUR
(Antecedent: cue before the behaviour)	(Behaviour observed or wanted)

Puppy Training Practice Schedules

Practising each skill regularly is key to reliable behaviours and ongoing learning and success for you and your puppy or dog. Below are weekly ideas of training schedules to follow. As puppy and dog owners we understand that sometimes life events and work affect our lives and therefore our dogs lives too, whether that is illness or a holiday and we need to take breaks from dog training. These are not strict training schedules, but ideas of how long to practice and when to add in training times, socialising to the world and enrichment.

Each week comes with a challenge which was created for our in-person clients, with the added incentive of completing the challenge and winning treats. However, for owners following this course at home without in person training, we always enjoy receiving emails and puppy photos. We may not be able to send you treats but are always happy to inspire and encourage you and your puppy learning together.

Week One Puppy Training Schedule

The key to teaching and likewise learning, is to move at the learner's pace and slowly build new behaviours. Dog trainers will often speak about the "three Ds" in training: duration, distance, and distraction. Each of these represents a set of challenges for the dog. Gradually increasing the criteria, the time you ask the dog for a behaviour, for example a 'touch', then marking that duration with a click or marker word, adding your reinforcement increases duration. (Food for e.g.) Distance we increase by slowly moving away from the dog and asking for the 'touch' behaviour. We can add distraction by practising in different environments. We always raise our criteria by changing 1 'D' at a time. So, if increasing duration, practice in a quiet, known environment.

Week One	Training and Enrichment Schedule
Week 1 we're focusing on reflex to name, capturing eye contact and building engagement. We are also looking at scent-based activities on walks and at home to build confidence. Plus, aiding warm-ups and cool- downs before and after walks. Introducing a marker word or clicker to shape behaviour. On walks carry treats, stop at benches and let your puppy watch different stimuli, scooters, people with umbrellas, children on bikes, cars etc and then sprinkle some	• Ditch the food bowl, use a snufflemat, Kong, egg boxes, find it trails. • Freework- 3 x per week. (Treats in a ball pit/egg boxes set up to choose from a variety) • Prior to a walk set up a set activity for your puppy. A cardboard box with tissue and treat layers she can snuffle through. If a larger box hid toys as well as treats. • Sniffari Walks! Use a longer lead and go for a scent led walk- 3 x per week. • Keep rewarding reflex to name daily.

treats. Bikes/children = good things happen. This is an important part of socialisation.

Harness and lead desensitisation:
Having your puppy feel comfortable and relaxed when equipment is put on is important. Work on desensitising your puppy separately to walks. Once your puppy has the harness on comfortably, play a game in the garden. This will decrease arousal prior to walks. Harness = walk, play in the garden, scent activity.

Training Treat Tip: Buy treats that can be broken up into tiny pieces, this will reduce the size of each treat for rapid rewarding, while teaching new behaviours.

Puppy's Name = treats/food/play (Good things).
This will help recall.

- Capture and reward eye contact. Puppy looks at you = reward.

- Introduce your puppy to different environments, textures, sights, people, bikes, scooters, mobility aids, children, other dogs slowly. We are looking for positive experiences during puppy development. Think quality over quantity.

- Harness Desensitisation x 5 reps this week.

- Make notes on body language changes and when they occur.

Week Two Puppy Training Schedule

Week Two	Training and Enrichment Schedule
Week 2 we're focusing on teaching a reliable 'Drop' cue, capturing wanted behaviour around food, what to do about jumping up and polite greetings. **1st Challenge!** Settle with your puppy in a new environment this week! Send me a photo or video by WhatsApp or email showing a settle in a new environment or space, and you will get some training treats if we are seeing you in person for training classes or 1-2-1. Each week will have a new challenge with the last leading to a great extra. Practice behaviours for 3-5 minutes and end on a success!	- Ditch the food bowl, use a snufflemat, Kong, egg boxes, find it trails. - Freework- 3 x per week. (Treats in a ball pit/egg boxes set up to choose from a variety) - Prior to a walk set up a set activity for your puppy. A cardboard box with tissue and treat layers she can snuffle through. If a larger box hid toys as well as treats. - Reinforce calm behaviour and paws on the floor which is rewarded. Ignore jumping up so that your dog learns that this does not pay. You can teach a default sit when you approach people.

We are also looking at scent-based activities on walks and at home to build confidence. Plus, aiding warm-ups and cool- downs before and after walks. Introducing a marker word or clicker to shape behaviour. On walks carry treats, stop at benches, and let your puppy watch different stimuli, scooters, people with umbrellas, children on bikes, cars etc and then sprinkle some treats. Bikes/children = good things happen. This is an important part of socialisation. Sniffari Walks! Use a longer lead and go for a scent led walk- 3 x per week. Introduce your puppy to different environments, textures, sights, people, children, other dogs slowly. We are looking for positive experiences during puppy development. Think quality over quantity.	• Practice the Food Manners game x 3 reps. • Practice the drop tug game x 3 reps. • Work on settling daily, building duration on a mat/blanket. Your challenge is having your puppy settled in a new environment. That could be outside in your garden while you have a coffee, your kitchen while you prepare lunch, in a cafe or a dog friendly store, or the pub. Remember about your 3 D's, distance, duration and distraction. (This is a lot for our puppies and a 5-minute settle is great at this stage.) • Keep rewarding reflex to name daily. Name = treats/food/play (Good things). This will help recall. • Capture and reward eye contact. Puppy looks at you = reward. • Harness Desensitisation x 3 reps this week. • Make notes on body language changes and when they occur.

Week Three Puppy Training Schedule

Week Three	Training and Enrichment Schedule
Week 3 we're focusing on recall and engagement, including loose lead foundations. **2nd Challenge!** Teach a Hand Target! Send me a photo or video by WhatsApp or email showing your hand target with a little distance, and you will get some training treats if we are seeing you in person for training classes or 1-2-1. Each week will	• Ditch the food bowl, use a snufflemat, Kong, egg boxes, find it trails. • Freework- 3 x per week. (Treats in a ball pit/egg boxes set up to choose from a variety) • Prior to a walk set up a set activity for your puppy. A cardboard box with tissue

have a new challenge with the last leading to a great extra.

We are also looking at scent-based activities on walks and at home to build confidence. Plus, aiding warm-ups and cool- downs before and after walks. Plus, looking at building our settling, increasing duration, distance and distraction.

On walks carry treats, stop at benches and let your puppy watch different stimuli, scooters, people with umbrellas, children on bikes, cars etc and then sprinkle some treats. Bikes = good things happen.

- and treat layers she can snuffle through. If a larger box hid toys as well as treats.
- Sniffari Walks! Use a longer lead and go for a scent led walk- 3 x per week.
- Practice the Counting Game x 5 reps for 5 mins per session. Try this in the home then build to outside space.
- Keep rewarding reflex to name daily.
- Practise your recall cue in the home at short distances and then build slowly.
- Practise the lead skills from our session: for owners following this class guide at home, keep capturing eye contact and engagement.
- Make notes on body language changes and when they occur.
- Work on your hand target x 3 reps for 5 mins.
- Keep practicing your drop cue, try different trades this week.
- Food Manners Game x 3 reps for 5 mins per session. Reward wanted behaviour around food.
- Work on settling daily x 5 mins and slowly increase duration. Pick a time when your puppy is more tired and relaxed.

Week Four Puppy Training Schedule

Week Four	Training and Enrichment Schedule
Week 4 we're focusing on teaching and building a 'Stay' cue, how we use eye contact to teach a 'Leave' and loose lead skills.	• Ditch the food bowl, use a snufflemat, Kong, egg boxes, find it trails. • Freework- 3 x per week.

3rd Challenge! Send me a photo or video by WhatsApp or email showing you training a 'stay' cue with a little distance away from you, and you will get some training treats if we are seeing you in person for training classes or 1-2-1. Each week will have a new challenge with the last leading to a great extra.

We are also looking at scent-based activities on walks and at home to build confidence. Plus, aiding warm-ups and cool- downs before and after walks. Plus, looking at building our settling, increasing duration, distance and distraction.

On walks carry treats, stop at benches and let your puppy watch different stimuli, scooters, people with umbrellas, children on bikes, cars etc and then sprinkle some treats. Bikes = good things happen.

Build the loose lead skills and training into every walk, for part of the walk. This may be easier in a quiet area on your daily walk, or on the way home. Begin by marking and rewarding engagement, eye contact and check-ins.

(Treats in a ball pit/egg boxes set up to choose from a variety)

- Prior to a walk set up a set activity for your puppy. A cardboard box with tissue and treat layers she can snuffle through. If a larger box hid toys as well as treats.
- Sniffari Walks! Use a longer lead and go for a scent led walk- 3 x per week.
- Keep rewarding reflex to name daily.
- Practice your 'Stay' training, building distance away from your dog slowly, building distance will also be adding duration. If you find your puppy is moving, go back a few steps x 3 reps for 5 mins.
- Work on teaching your leave cue x 3 reps for 5 mins. Remember the 3 'Ds'!
- Practise the lead skills daily from our session: for owners following this class guide at home, keep capturing eye contact and engagement.
- Make notes on body language changes and when they occur.
- Continue to work on your hand target x 3 reps for 5 mins and building your recall cue. Use the counting game on walks and new environments.
- Keep practicing your drop cue, continuing with different trades.
- Food Manners Game x 3 reps for 5 mins per session. Reward wanted behaviour around food.
- Work on settling daily x 5 mins and slowly increase duration. Pick a time

Week Five Puppy Training Schedule

Week Five	Training and Enrichment Schedule
	when your puppy is more tired and relaxed.
Week 5 we're focusing on husbandry and cooperative care for grooming, vet visits and day to day care. **4th Challenge!** Send me a photo or video by WhatsApp or email showing you teaching the 'Bucket Game' with your puppy, and you will get some training treats if we are seeing you in person for training classes or 1-2-1. Each week will have a new challenge with the last leading to a great extra. We are also looking at scent-based activities on walks and at home to build confidence. Plus, aiding warm-ups and cool- downs before and after walks. Also, looking at building our settling, increasing duration, distance and distraction. On walks carry treats, stop at benches and let your puppy watch different stimuli, scooters, people with umbrellas, children on bikes, cars etc and then sprinkle some treats. Bikes = good things happen. Build the loose lead skills and training into every walk, for part of the walk. This may be easier in a quiet area on your daily walk, or on the way home. Begin by marking and rewarding engagement, eye contact and check-ins.	• Ditch the food bowl, use a snufflemat, Kong, egg boxes, find it trails. • Freework- 3 x per week. (Treats in a ball pit/egg boxes set up to choose from a variety) • Prior to a walk set up a set activity for your puppy. A cardboard box with tissue and treat layers she can snuffle through. If a larger box hid toys as well as treats. • Sniffari Walks! Use a longer lead and go for a scent led walk- 3 x per week. • Keep rewarding reflex to name daily. • Practise the lead skills daily from our session: for owners following this class guide at home, keep capturing eye contact and engagement. Plus, work on the 'follow me' loose lead skill x 5 reps for 5 mins. • Muzzle Training x 3 reps for 5 mins. • Practice 'Stand' x 3 reps for 5 mins. • Bucket Game: wait for a quiet time where you can relax with your puppy, dog and introduce this game comfortably. Remember this game is a conversation between you and your puppy. • Make notes on body language changes and when they occur.

	• Work on your hand target x 3 reps for 5 mins and introduce as part of recall on your walks, along with the counting game.
	• Keep practicing your drop and leave cues with different items and trading.
	• Food Manners Game x 3 reps for 5 mins per session. Reward wanted behaviour around food.
	• Continue working on your 'Stay' by building distance and duration away from your puppy, dog.
	• Work on settling daily x 5 mins and slowly increase duration. Pick a time when your puppy is more tired and relaxed.

Week Six Puppy Training Schedule

Week Six	Training and Enrichment Schedule
Week 6 we're focusing on all learnt skills and building each foundation. **Last Challenge!** Send me a photo or video by WhatsApp or email showing you training loose lead on a walk with a lovely, relaxed lead, and if we are seeing you in person for training classes or 1-2-1, we can meet up for an additional training walk and catch up. This will give you a chance to talk through any concerns and to help you move into adolescence with your puppy. We are also looking at scent-based activities on walks and at home to build confidence. Plus, aiding warm-ups and cool- downs before and after walks.	• Ditch the food bowl, use a snufflemat, Kong, egg boxes, find it trails. Enrichment for our dogs is as important as training new skills. • Freework- 3 x per week. (Treats in a ball pit/egg boxes set up to choose from a variety) • Prior to a walk set up a set activity for your puppy. A cardboard box with tissue and treat layers she can snuffle through. If a larger box hid toys as well as treats. • Sniffari Walks! Use a longer lead and go for a scent led walk- 3 x per week.

Plus, looking at building our settling, increasing duration, distance and distraction.

On walks carry treats, stop at benches and let your puppy watch different stimuli, scooters, people with umbrellas, children on bikes, cars etc and then sprinkle some treats. Bikes = good things happen.

Practice each skill for 3-5 minutes and always end the training session on success! Do not be afraid to go back over training skills or go back a few steps.

- Work on settling daily x 5 mins and slowly increase duration. Pick a time when your puppy is more tired and relaxed. By now you and your puppy will be working on longer duration and our aim is for your puppy, dog to be settled while you make a cup of tea and sit down. You will also be taking a blanket, mat out with you for stops on walks perhaps in a café and where your puppy can safely and comfortably rest.

- Loose Lead Skills are key to enjoy your walks over the lifetime and adventures with your dogs. A doll that pulls can cause injuries to a handler, particularly your wrists, arms and shoulders as well as a risk of being pulled over. As an owner and handler of sled dog breeds, this is a skill I work on daily with my puppies, fosters and adopted dogs. Loose lead walking is a skill that takes time, but pays with years of enjoyable walks, focus and engagement.

- Recall Skills: Practice in different environments once reliable in low distraction. Always use a long line on a harness to prevent neck injuries. A long line will prevent unwanted behaviour of ignoring a recall cue occurring and being practised. Longlines are great management for training and in new environments that a puppy or dog does not know well, keeping them safe.

About the Book and Course

All worksheets, including this puppy course guide/book are owned by Suzanne Man-Ray and not to be shared without permission. They are for guidance for dog owner clients of the Wolf and Whippet.

If you have any concerns, questions or need support please contact us by phone, message via Whatsapp or email. Keep in touch during the course if you are working with us 1-2-1 or via classes and send us videos of progress. If you need any further video demos during classes and 1-2-1 support, please let us know as these can be sent via WhatsApp. For owners following this guide at home and need further support I work remotely with clients over the UK and internationally.

Dog Training may produce desired results quickly, although it is generally the case that time, commitment and consistency is required. Implementing the dog training plan remains the owner's responsibility at all times.

Suzy Man-Ray – Wolf and Whippet Dog Training

wolfandwhippet@gmail.com

www.wolfandwhippet.com

Wolf and Whippet promote reward-based training. We only use **positive, reward-based training methods**, no punishment and firmly stand with the **Pet Professionals Guild's** ethos of No Pain, No Force, No Fear. The methods we use are force-free, looking at current scientific research, using positive reinforcement, classical and operant conditioning.

We want to offer clients a safe space and ongoing support that we would want throughout a puppy's development and dog's life. Our training support and care also includes enrichment and scent-based games which we incorporate into all of our work.

About Your Trainer and Author

Suzy is a certified trainer by INTODogs and ICAN. She is a member of the PPG and only uses reward-based training methods. Suzy has a passion for rescue and has fostered and worked for various rescues. Suzy enjoys teaching husbandry and cooperative care, alongside supporting dog owners with training, creating individual training plans. Suzy was inspired by her dog Okami, an Alaskan Malamute to begin studying training and behaviour and continues to learn through yearly continual professional development and practical courses.

Suzy is also an accredited Hoopers Instructors with Canine Hoopers UK and Hoopers World.

REFERENCES

Emily J. Blackwell, John W. S. Bradshaw, Rachel A. Casey, Fear responses to noises in domestic dogs: Prevalence, risk factors and co-occurrence with other fear related behaviour, Applied Animal Behaviour Science, Volume 145. Issues 1–2, April 2013, Pages 15-25, 2013

Nancy A. Dreschel, Douglas A. Granger Physiological and behavioural reactivity to stress in thunderstorm-phobic dogs and their caregivers, Applied Animal Behaviour Science, Volume 95. Issues 3-4, December 2005, Pages 153-168, 2005

Angelika Firnkes, Angela Bartels, Emilie Bidoli, Michael Erhard, Appeasement signals used by dogs during dog–human communication, Journal of Veterinary Behaviour, Volume 19, 2017.

Landsberg. G, Hunthausen. W, Ackerman. L, Handbook of Behaviour Problems of the Dog and Cat, 2008

Panksepp, J et al. (1978) The biology of social attachments: opiates alleviate separation distress.

Panksepp J. (1998). Affective Neuroscience: The Foundations of Human and Animal Emotions. New York, NY: Oxford University Press.

Pongracz, Peter. (2014) Social Learning In Dogs. The Social Dog. Elsevier Academic Press

Schnade, V. (2009) Bonding With Your Dog.

Serpell, James. (2018) The Domestic Dog. Cambridge University Press

Schnade, V. (2009) Bonding With Your Dog.

Stewart, Grisha. (2016) Behaviour Adjustment Training 2.0. Dogwise Publication

Pongracz, Peter. (2014) Social Learning In Dogs. The Social Dog. Elsevier Academic Press

Storengen, L.M., Lingaas, F. Noise sensitivity in 17 dog breeds: prevalence, breed risk and correlation with fear in other situations. Applied Animal Behaviour Science, 2015

Tiffani J Howell, Tammie King, Pauleen C Bennett, Dove Press journal: Veterinary Medicine: Research and Reports. Puppy parties and beyond: the role of early age socialization practices on adult dog behaviour, 2015.

PHOTO/IMAGE REFERENCES

Figure 1 – Canine Emotional Development by Suzanne Man-Ray

Figure 2 – Stress Triggers and Threshold by Suzanne Man-Ray

Figure 3 – Trigger Stacking and Threshold by Suzanne Man-Ray

Figure 4 - Classical Conditioning by Suzanne Man-Ray

NOTES

Behaviour Chain: Chaining is an approach in dog training that combines two or more behaviours to create a whole chain, often added to one cue. A behaviour chain involves breaking down and teaching small individual steps of a behaviour separately.

Forward Chaining: involves the puppy or dog learning to chain a series of behaviours, usually in an from the first to the last behaviour in the chain. The behaviours are trained in the order in which they are carried out.

This often the most logical way for people to learn and can be easily taught. However, often dogs can become frustrated trying to learn a new behaviour after a well-rewarded and rehearsed behaviour, causing frustration.

Back Chaining: the puppy or dog is taught the last behaviour of the chain first, then the behaviour before that, moving in a backwards order of the chain. For example, if teaching a dog to tidy toys into a basket, you would start by teaching the dog to drop into the basket first and reward with a high rate of reinforcement, before teaching other parts of chain. This will give the dog a high rate of success and reinforcement of the behaviour, making it reliable. This will mean as you add further steps to the chain you will always end on a success, a familiar behaviour, lowering frustration in training.

However, back chaining does have some disadvantages, and some dogs may skip steps in the chain, which may mean you need to go back a few steps and make each part of the chain reliable through reinforcement.

Note: You can also train a chain of behaviours from the middle of the chain out, where you add behaviours to the front and the back of the chain, gradually making it longer. For longer chains, especially in competitions, trainers may use a combination of forward and back chaining.

Last Training Tip!

Keep a box of novel toys in a cupboard away from your puppy or dog, tug toys, ropes, scent-based toys and high value treats. This will be your high value, novel box of fun things you revolve and pick from to take out on a walk with you. Not only will the environment be exciting now, but you will be too, as each walk you will have something new and fun, to reinforce desired behaviours such as a speedy recall away from another dog. Your puppy or dog will learn that when released off-lead or on a training long-line, you are the focus of fun and play, not just other dogs, squirrels, and the environment.

All information within in this puppy course guide is intellectual property of Suzanne Man-Ray, presented by Suzy (Intodogs accredited). This printed document/book is not to be shared or copied without permission. The document was originally created in 2018 based on Wolf and Whippet's 1-2-1 Puppy course and is continually updated and changed. This latest copy was edited in 2022.

Photos within book – All photos are owned and the property of Suzanne Man-Ray.

Printed in Great Britain
by Amazon